The Left Hook

Danger: Do not read this book if you are a part of management or supervision.

The Left Hook

A funny adventure story on the shop floor

Charlie Reed

Order this book online at www.trafford.com
or email orders@trafford.com

Most Trafford titles are also available at major online book retailers.

Printed in the United States of America.

ISBN: 978-1-4269-9547-7 (sc)
ISBN: 978-1-4269-9588-0 (e)

Library of Congress Control Number: 2011916816

Trafford rev. 12/06/2011

 www.trafford.com

North America & international
toll-free: 1 888 232 4444 (USA & Canada)
phone: 250 383 6864 ♦ fax: 812 355 4082

In this story, the names and places have been changed to protect the infamous.

Cঙ

Working in the factory was no easy job. The environment, the management and the work was very difficult. I first worked in general machines. This is where we would repair bearings that did not meet customer requirements. One night I was working on the press stamping parts and I looked over and saw the boss. He was looking through the garbage cans, so I stopped what I was doing and walked over and asked him. What were you looking for, and he told me , he couldn't stop now to talk because he was looking for a bomb ! Apparently someone had called in a bomb scare. But what management failed to do is clear the plant before the search. Instead, they left us all working at our workstations, while they searched the plant. I went to the union steward and told him we should be all evacuated. He said next time maybe we can convince management that we needed to evacuate the plant first because if there was a bomb in the plant, that's the last place we want to be. They ended up catching the person that was calling in the bomb scares. They traced the phone call to the lobby of the plant where there were three phone booths right across from the personnel department. So, the next time he called in a bomb scare. They traced the call and walked out the door and caught him and put him in handcuffs. I think he did five years in prison, but I'm not sure. My next job was in the heat treating process. It had a large furnace, which management had to shut down on the weekends if we were not working. I worked second shift, so I watched management take their instruction book and go around turning knobs and turning off the gas to the furnace. The foreman would get to a certain place in the process, and all of a sudden, you heard a large, and I mean a large bang from the furnace, which would blow off the top three vents and scare everybody out of their wits in the area. Now this happened for years, to all new people that were reading the manual book. Little did they know two of the operations were backwards. So, if you followed the directions as called for in the SOP, the furnace would emit a loud bang. We didn't know this, but we did know that all new people would make the furnace explode. Normally, we had other things to do, while the foreman shut off the furnace. One day, I followed a foreman around and walked through the process with him and found the mistake and ask him to change it in the book before the next person shut the furnace down. When he changed it in the SOP, "standard operating procedure". There were no more loud bangs at the end of the shift on Friday nights. While I was training in heat treat on first shift Friday, the foreman came around to give us our paychecks. The older worker, I was training with handed his paycheck back to the foreman and said "this check isn't right get it straightened out" and then he would give it back to him. When I asked him why he gave his paycheck back to the foreman he said. I do that about every other week, and they come back with more money every time. So I know they're cheating me. The company had us on an incentive plan , the more bearings we produced the more we would be paid. But most workers didn't know how to calculate that formula. So they would just hand their paychecks back and demanded that it be recalculated, just another interesting fact about factory life, I learned. In the heat treat department. It was hot. 106° at the drinking fountain. The company put fans, large fans, which made large blowing noises and this would blow around black soot and smoke and we couldn't wait to get off work. We would be covered at night when we went home with soot, sweat and oil mist from the grinding departments. No showers were available at that time, they were later installed, so workers could take a shower before they went home. Some people would go the locker room before work, change into their work clothes, and after work would shower and change into their street clothes.

After a few years, I signed into the grind areas, we had this certain supervisor that would go around turning up all of the pressure on the machines to make the machines go faster. The cycle times would be 16 seconds and the manufacturer said the machines were engineered to run at 32 seconds per part. I worked second shift on this bank of machines, and I would slow the cycle down and turn down the pressure. So the machines would run much better without repairing them all night long, I would get more parts at the end of the shift. Old-timers on day shift noticed this that I wasn't having as much trouble as they were on day shift and one setup person asked how I was doing it. I didn't want to tell him at first, because I didn't know if I could trust him. I didn't want him running to the supervisor and telling them that I was turning down the machines. But after five or six months of talking to this old-timer. I felt sorry for them because they're working so hard on day shift. I told him as soon as day shift leaves, I would go to every machine and turn down the pressure to 200 instead of 240. He said you got to be kidding me. I can't believe you're doing that. I said no, that's how I get so many parts and my quality was better than anybody's. After we finished talking, I saw him go directly into the foreman's office. And I saw them pointing in the direction of the department. When I came in the next day. The supervisor caught me as I was coming into the department and told me he didn't want me to turn down the pressure on the machines anymore, but I told him the machines run better, and I don't have to repair them all night like day shift does. He said if I ever turn them down again he would fire me. This stupervisor cost the company more money than any one person ever did, millions, I think. We had a pet name for this stupervisor, Neal-down. He got this name, because he went over to a through feed machine and knelt down to try to catch a bug in a drip pan, but it wasn't a bug. It was the air from the motor from the machine blowing on the oil in the drip pan. He knelt down with the pan card in his hand and was fishing through the oily mess.

This book was written in part by newsletters. Wrote and distributed weekly on the shop floor. We wrote the newsletters to make fun of management. We put out the newsletter weekly, and I say we because fellow workers would contribute articles and cartoons. So we put out the newsletters together but before we get to the newsletter articles. I want to tell you a few more things that happened on the shop floor. The supervisors had been complaining about workers, not being on the job on time. One day I saw this young worker, tying his boots before work, but as luck would have it, his shoelace broke, so he went up to the locker room to get new laces. When he came back the supervisor asked him why he wasn't on the job on time. The worker explained how his shoelace broke, but the supervisor took the worker to the front office and fired him and escorted him to the front gate. Training in this department was very bad. You had to learn everything on your own if you are going to be good at what you do. I finally signed out of that department, but I always went back to help out the younger guys that were learning. The company had gotten new machines in and management wanted workers to train on the new machines. On Saturday, and they said they would buy pizza for everyone. One worker was complaining to me that he didn't like pizza. So when I found out all about the story. I told the worker I can take care of that, if you don't mind. So I went in to the personnel department and told them. It was a violation of Wage Hour Laws to work three or four hours for pizza. So that was that, the workers got paid. In this same department, we would have wrecks on the machines bad ones, real bad. Sometimes they would have fires and some workers would even quit instead of staying there and working in that environment. The mist was bad in that area and some peoples skin was breaking out, some workers wore bread bags on their hands and arms to protect them. But it only made things worse. We tried to get the cutting fluid, l,l,l, trichloroethane, recycled into 55 gallon drums. But that took over two years, and even then workers would continue to pour the cutting fluid into the machines, why I'll never know. But that was life on the shop floor, but we were no angels. We would throw rags at each other to kill the boredom but then, everything would get out of hand, as usual, and someone would start throwing rags with bearings it ,if it hit the machines right or wrong the machines would wreck. One night a few workers made a football out of some rags and was playing in the aisle way. Well, as luck would have it. The supervisor came along and took them to the front office. It wouldn't have been a big problem, but one of the workers broke the window in the personnel office. And when they fired him. He went out into the parking lot and scratched up the supervisor's new truck. What a night that was.

Before I get into the articles in the newsletters I want to say something about the union in the plant or lack of it. We took it upon ourselves to help ourselves and others in a bad spot with the company, the union was always there to support the company in every thing management did. So, we learned to put out a newsletter to say what we felt and to make fun of management. But I would give you one warning, if you try a newsletter in your workplace, don't get caught! You know, what could happen. So if you don't know who you're working with don't try it.

"I'm working smarter, not harder!"

Reality check—Inspection gets a new pricey piece of equipment, and the company can have a hole knocked in the wall and have a door put in. But when we want a sign, put on a door to remind fellow workers. There are hazardous chemicals being used, ill-Pill says no. And when our health and safety representative puts up his own sign, ill-Pill says no and takes it down. The company cares more about how it looks then about how it affects us. They must figure there is no problem if there is no sign. But then, that is why Pill is Ill, in the head.

Two-Faced, Too Much—Lately, the supervisor's have been real chummy, joining us for breaks and lunches. A few of us have even gotten some coffee out of them. Why are they so palsey-walsey? Maybe higher management, told them to get lost. Or maybe they found out, what we have known all along. It is easier to talk to someone with only one face !!!

$4000 Reward—Recently, a collection was raised to help find a daughter of one of the workers here. Nearly $4000 was raised. When workers come together and act to help each other. We can do a lot more, than if, we would act separately.

It's all for Show—We want to tell the health and safety representative, who quit the safety committee, recently. We understand his frustrations. The company is more concerned on how things look to the tour groups. Then how things really are. Remember the fire brigade? It's a mirage. Remember the nurse we were going to get? Another tall tale. Remember the safety committee? It's almost dead. Since it doesn't work for us. It must be for show. So move it to Hollywood !!!

<u>Health and Safety, What a joke</u>—For all the people who are not concerned about health and safety at the company. Don't worry about it, the company is not either, the way it goes now. Big cheese and Ill-Pill control health and safety meetings. That's why nothing ever gets done. It's pretty sad, that they have a problem informing people on certain chemicals in the plant. But our right to know about safety is what it's all about.

<u>Looking for Something</u>—Running machines through breaks and lunches doesn't always add up to more production. If Wimmy wants us to do it he might find out the hard way that you get less but whatever you do, don't stand in the way of production. Wimmy might get pissed-off. Wimmy must have gone to stupervisor school and they told him he is so wonderful. He knows how to make a decision, so now he's going around, looking for one he can make!

<u>Fair pay</u>—Recently the company handed out cards describing plant policy and goals, one supposed policy is that the company pays fair. But why do we get no profit-sharing checks at the same time, Big Scary announces the company made big enough profits. To make large new investments? Why do we have a $30 Blue Cross co-pay? Why are there no company contributions to the 401K plan? Yeah, they pay fair — bus fare, just barely.

<u>A good start</u>—The employee who was recently fired for allegedly pushing a foreman, should not have lost a days work. We have been getting "pushed" for years, it's about time we start pushing back.

Ill-Pills Tricks—The company started 10 new workers recently. Two were relatives of the Union officials. Of course all of our relatives, a job here would be better than a job at Fast Food Store. But it's rotten of the company to try to divide us by hiring only a certain type of relative and filtering out the rest. And it does divide us if we get mad at those who were hired. Its not their fault, it is the company's fault for getting many workers competing for 10 measly jobs. 10 more jobs is 10 more jobs. But we could use a lot more help around here, all the overtime we're working shows that.

Who's a thief?—Long-John put up a notice about thefts in the plant, of people's personal belongings. Long-John calls the people responsible either sick or stupid. For sure workers stealing from other workers is not cool. But there is an even bigger thief to deal with. The company steals wealth from our labor every day.

Sick or Stupid — Both!—Long-John shouldn't be one to call others sick or stupid. When he is well known to the women of the plant to make disgusting and degrading remarks about them. Above all, his remarks are both sick and stupid.

New weight-loss plan?—Since there is no more a eating in the front office, it has been rough on the fat cats, and the cafeteria. The fat cats are screwing up the economy again — donuts sales are plummeting !

They call this Safe?—We make bearings, and we need to work with oils of all kinds. But the company needs to find oils that don't produce dermatitis. If that's impossible we want lost-time pay and should be off work until it's completely cleared up. Apparently, the company doesn't feel it's a big problem and why should they? They don't have to work in it.

<u>Our money or his job</u>—Why does G.I. Joe gets so excited when we catch him in a lie? That's what happens when he gets caught. Scheduling over time in the sort pool can't be that hard. When he makes a mistake. He lies about it. It costs us money. You would think it was costing him his job.

<u>Don't believe the hype</u>—Did anybody catch the fine print on bumper stickers that were passed out recently? "Do not display on an import", it said. As if imports are the problem! We have been told time after time that if we only support the company we work for, buy from them. Take cutbacks, anything to make them profits then we'll all do okay. But what happened? Companies right here have made big profits. And they're still laying off still cutting wages and benefits Foreign workers aren't the enemy. They aren't the ones taking our jobs. The bosses we work for the bosses right here, that's who our fight is with.

<u>Stingy Santa</u>—Christmas is coming and we are having a Christmas raffle to raise money for people who don't have jobs. Again, we need jobs for all of us, not charity, but we can't expect the bosses to put that in our stockings.

<u>Moving but not far enough</u>—Recently the cheering in a department could be heard all the way to the airport. When workers heard that the supervisor was being moved to shipping. We couldn't contain our joy. But the only problem now is that shipping workers have to deal with Her big head. If higher management

was going to move her. Why did they have to stop at shipping? It's not that cold outside. Management must have figured they are saving training costs, because as everyone knows. She knows everything, including the size of her ego.

<u>Are they twins?</u>—Hey kneel—down, was that you on TV or is David Duke your brother?

<u>A workers quote</u>—You can either believe what the company says. Or you can read the truth in the newsletter. We couldn't have said it better!
<u>They make the Rules</u>—We have a question. What is the MOA program and process referred to in our new contract books? We must maintain full commitment to it, then why weren't we given the full details of the program. It sounds like they're going to make it up as they go along. That's nothing new. That's what the company has been doing for years!!

<u>Chair wars</u>—Eachy, Eachy, Eachy is doing it again. He's taking our chairs away and throwing them out. But we only use them to sit on. So, throw out all you want Eachy it won't hurt us. We'll sit on the floor if we have to. If the company really wants to empower us and wants us to take more responsibility, then if we want a chair to sit on. We should get a chair, period! Someone better get that loose cannon off our ass, now. Or you can kiss MOA goodbye.

<u>Horsing around</u>—A couple weeks ago, some supervisors read us the riot act about horseplay in the plant, of course just a little while later Party Animal was seen pinching Peter rabbit on the butt. These

supervisors keep a separate set of rules for themselves and the first one, is do as I say not as I do!

The heat is on—Seems that party animal still can't handle the heat. He was seen in his office with a fan on, must still be negotiating.

Huff and Puff—Ill-Pill fired another worker, a couple of weeks ago. He couldn't come up with a good reason. So he made something up. When management found out they quickly overturned his action. Even they could see the stupidity of his action!

Jitter season—Deer season is coming up soon. Just because the company is selling 600,000 bearings a day doesn't mean that the company should get the jitters, because we take a couple of days off. It happens every year, so they should be used to it by now.

We're better off without them—Management runs around like a bunch of babbling supervisors trying to nail us for every little thing we do wrong. It seems they're trying to get something on us. So they have something to hold over our heads. No wonder we run better production on the weekends.

Personal is Personal—When you're out sick and come back with a doctor's note. Now, they go directly to the nurse, why? So she can call the doctor and pump him for information. Some people think your medical problems are personal, and no one else's business, but not the company.

Cost savings?—Management says that they are on a cost-saving mission. That's why we got the new soap, but if they are so big on cost savings. Why do they spare no expense when it comes to having lots of supervisors and engineers? Why are they spending $24 million on a new plant out of state? And why are they working many of us seven days and 12 hours a day? We don't see much cost savings in that!

<u>What are they afraid of?</u>—Voluntary overtime, some workplaces already have it and it works out fine for the company and the workers. But maybe we can get voluntary overtime on our next contract. If the bosses can see their way through their fear of losing control.

<u>Boss Free and Free Speech</u>—Does upper management know why the plant runs better production on the weekends? It's because we don't have a lot of supervisors running around holding us up. There are too many bosses. We don't need that many, and even some bosses will admit to that. If you get them alone!

<u>"Working" a Sunday?</u>—Eachy came into the plant last Sunday! On a weekend!. He did the <u>usual</u> thing. We hope he didn't lie to his wife and say he worked a Sunday!

<u>New system, "stalking machines"</u>—Have you ever seen an engineer stand with their hands-on there hips or with their arms crossed, and just stare at the machine for an hour or two. You may be thinking they are trying to kill time or asleep while standing, but they're really not, what they're really doing is what's called "stalking machines". With this system, engineers stand and stare at the machines to be repaired, and one of two things will happen, first, if he stands there long enough

the machine may fix itself, two, a setup person will come over and help fix it!

20 cents—we get $.20 for a raise this week. You can't even buy a replacement water pumped for that and you know, we're going to all need one if Eachy has his way with quality.

Our COLA's is in their pockets—Once again were not getting a COLA increase this September. Why? It was sucked up by our pensions. The pensions we have to pay for, ever since our last contract. Of course we all need a good pension. But why should we have to pay for it. We pay for it every day, year in and year out every day we were in here making big profits for the company.

One Continental break—For most of us, we work about seven hours a day two breaks and our lunch is about an hour a day. But how is it that we see an engineer in the cafeteria all the time, all day long. How many hours a day or a week does he work since he is an engineer. Why doesn't management give them a job like discovering a way we could run our machines and sit in the cafeteria at the same time!

Management logic—Eachy doesn't want time spent to rework bad parts in assembly. So what does he do. He goes through and pulls all the reject tickets from the bad parts. But that just makes more work for the operators anyway, because they have to deal with working with bad parts. Eachy is living in a fantasy world. He thinks that if you call a bad part good. It'll be good. He thinks if you cut corners over here, it won't catch up with you later on. He probably believes Santa Claus will bring him something for nothing too!

Our Absences are reasonable—Chucky Please is ordering the supervisors to write up workers for absenteeism. Based on his standards, but those standards are based on a five day week. Most of us work six and seven days a week. 12 occurrences in a year might seem like a lot based on 40 hours, five days a week. In fact, it's a lot less since we are all cramming two weeks of work into one.

Missed a few—After all the time Banana Mike spent writing up the new break and launch schedule. He still neglected a few breaks that we all take like :
    # 1 smoke breaks
    # 2 bathroom breaks
    # 3 get a mop break
    # 4 visit your co-worker break
    # 5 argue with eachy break
    # 6 Throw Wrench in the machine break
    # 7 get your supplies break
    # 8 get change break
    # 9 top of the hour break
    # 10 collect pop cans break
    # 11 plant wide meeting break
    # 12 give blood break
    # 13 morning meeting break
    # 14 go see the nurse break
    # 15 payroll error break
    # 16 safety problem break
    # 17 talk to the union break
    # 18 get a drink of water break
    # 19 take a shower break
    # 20 get a breath of fresh air break

\# 21 work on your machine break
\# 22 take the plant tour break
\# 23 phone call break
\# 24 read the paper break
\# 25 pick your teeth break

Mike, get back to the drawing board !

<u>Engineering at its best</u>—Another way to fix a ceiling leak is to put up a metal pan near the ceiling and run a hose down to a trash can presto, it's fixed.

<u>Too much stress</u>—A worker in a department had a heart attack, a couple weeks ago. How many people will have to get a heart attack before the company knows there is too much stress on the job. That's why we need all the breaks. If the company won't take care of the problem, we will !

<u>Janitors Jubilee</u>—This week another supervisor came back to hourly only after months of being jacked around by management. He finally made it. Now he is in a much better job, janitor in the utility department. It's not hard to understand why many people prefer it to a management job.

<u>Training time</u>—Management has been training the new supervisors for several weeks now. The question is how long will it take for us workers to train him? Guess it depends on how smart he is.

<u>You can't weasel out of this one</u>—Why was the party animal over in H4 messing with workers and ordering them around? Doesn't he know or is he really out of his mind? It appears party animal is trying to weasel

his way up to General supervisor, in the last newsletter we put party animal in W2. But he walks around in H4. So we don't misidentify him again. His last name begins with W.

Donut control—We've heard, there is a new policy, no more eating in the big front offices. So no more sneaking doughnuts in. Maybe they got tired of getting manuals with sticky goo all over them. Or maybe this is a new diet program for upper management, to make sure they can still fit in their chairs.

In an ideal world, in their dreams—This new absentee policy means that you can't have a family problem that needs attention. Since all absences are treated the same.
That's okay, all those with an ideal family, with no sudden illnesses or no crisis will have nothing to worry about ,whoops, that's right. Nobody's families is like that.

The right decision—A couple of supervisors have decided to come back to the union and we hear more are on the way. It's not surprising that the ones who are leaving management are the nicest. They must be the ones who are immune to rabies. At any rate, they made the right decision. Were sure that they have lots of funny little stories about being a stupervisor, break times should be entertaining for the next few weeks.

Discrimination or what?—It's good, the company has hired more workers. We need the help, but why do they hire only men workers. We know there are women out there who need jobs. So why aren't they ending up in here, does management have something against them or what ?

Stick it out then stick it to them—Warning to all probationary workers, another one has been fired. They make you kiss their ass for 90 days. It's a dirty job, but you have to do it. At least that long, after that, you can ignore management like the rest of us.

Not Wayward Wack-O—What do W3 and the stolen money from the cafeteria have in common? Well, lets see. Who's been breaking into toolboxes around the plant? Has anybody been caught, no. Has anyone admitted to it. Yes, W3 has ! What about breaking into lockers?. Has anybody been caught, no. Has anyone admitted to doing it yes W3 has ! Now who is in the immediate area of the cafeteria would you ask, you answer that.

Management in the way—In new H5 four workers have signed out to other jobs in the plant, these machines were supposed to solve our problems and be faster and easier to run, maybe management won't leave us alone to run the machines the way we know they can run quality parts. So, we signed out !

Are they crazy or what?—The figures came out recently for the last quarter's absenteeism, it was 4.1%. Well, heck the company only wants 3% so is the company crazy or what? It's instituted this new real restrictive absentee policy and it's gotten everyone up in arms and hot under the collar all for 1.1 lousy percent, that's only six hours per person, per quarter. Either they're crazy or 4.1% is a damn lie.

No-fault—The new absentee policies says if you are good this quarter, you get to take off
2 ½ days at the end of it . No fault after all! It's going to be lonely around here at the end of the month !

Be a team member—with the workers—Remember the day when Big Scary came into the plant to tell us the very same thing he had sent out a letter to tell us? And he talks about saving money! Why does he call us team members and say the company is our company? Because we do all the work, while he jet-sets around the world. We're starting to believe he used to work for the last plant manager.

No ifs ands or buts—W3 posted up the notice of vacation shutdown "but we'll know more if they finally decide". He says in "compliance with our labor agreement" we looked it up in the contract book and it doesn't say anything about ifs. But, that's why we have all those grievances, about all the ifs in W3's mind.

New solutions?—What are all those clear bed sheets doing hanging from the ceiling? Oh, that's just engineering's latest anti-leaking contribution! Well, don't worry Big—Scary, since they all look like bed sheets were sure no customer will notice them.

Management head games—Management is spreading rumors that the plant may close, again. Funny how all those rumors fly every time a contract or a union election comes up. Every time they want us to give up something, so what do they want us to give up now?

One week, what's the difference?—If the company is going to give us our holiday pay before the holidays why can't they give it to us even earlier like the 18th? That way we'd be able to do some gifts shopping with it. Guess that extra week of interest is important to them!

<u>A meal but no COLA's</u>—Last Tuesday was the annual retirees luncheon and a lot of retirees came, it's nice to see old friends again and see how they're doing. A meal once a year is nice with the pensions the way they are, with no COLA, some of them probably need the meal!

<u>Spreading that manure !</u>—Assembly line 20 ran some parts that were bad, bad, bad, at speed test but wouldn't you know it, quality management said ship them anyway. Quality boiled down to one thing, the opinion inside managements head. The bearings will be going on manure spreaders. That's appropriate since a lot of the manure was spread by saying that they're any good.

<u>Company of jugglers</u>—Profit sharing checks should be great this year with so many months of 100% production right? The management accountants have serious number juggling ahead of them to try and convince us of anything else.

<u>Plumbing can be complicated</u>—The ceiling was leaking in a spot so to fix it someone stuck a bucket right up in the rafters to catch the water. Then they attach to spigot to the bucket and ran a hose down into a garbage can. So now the leak is fixed. Gee—wouldn't <u>patching</u> the leak be easier. Some of these engineers have too much education and too much time on their hands.

Expensive policy—With this new absentee policy, the question is can management really afford the production lost that will come with it? You ask, what does that the absentee policy have to do with production? Wait and see . . .

We've seen them come and go—After all the havoc this policy will cause, who is still going to have their jobs, us or the people in personnel? And how many personnel people, have we lived through already?

Guaranteed profit maker—The new time clock ID cards will cost five dollars to replace them. So if enough people lose them. There is bound to be a profit next year !

Wayward Silly apologies—Why couldn't Wayward Silly keep his hands off someone else's toolbox? Why did he break into it? He's sorry alright, sorry he didn't find what he was looking for!

Someone's got to do it—While Eachy's hanging out at the bathrooms, why doesn't he make himself useful? The toilet seats could use a good cleaning, for starters. Next time you see Eachy gave him a can of spic n span!

Recycle Eachy, not!—Now that the company has its new trash compactor. There big on recycling, mainly because a company comes and gets the trash to pick through it for good stuff. They must love all those good used chairs that find their way into the trash can via Eachy.

Moneybags—Ever notice how when payroll errors are made in the company's favor, and they underpay us. They'll get to it "when they can", but on those few times when they are in our favor. Just watch how fast they moved to correct it. They'll even try to blame it on us. If they can move that fast, when it suits them. It just shows they can do the same for us. Maybe they just need a little encouragement!

Final audit blues—We need a sorting pool again. It shouldn't have been eliminated and why can't it be more voluntary? There are the those classifications that are not flooded with overtime. Why should it be based on who can holler the loudest. It looks like final rejects will be there for the next generation.

There is no point—Eachy thinks no one in the plant can give him a good argument on anything. We just don't try. You can't argue with an idiot. He never knows when he's lost.

An injury to one—A worker on second shift was badly injured recently when his arm was chewed up in a face grinder. This is a horrible thing to happen, and it's ironic it happened so close to Workers Memorial Day. This is what happens when people are under pressure to get the machines running as quickly as possible so that management can brag about being over 100%. No doubt about it the pace is responsible. And that means the company is responsible. It's not worth it to us to follow their pace.

The case of the missing chairs—Workers have been sorting all over the plant to clean up the rejects and get them out of the way for the end of the month and open house. And when chairs for sorting were in short supply. Workers got them from the front offices, if they want them back. They'll have to come and get them!

A new nurse—Recently first shift got a new nurse, as had been promised by management for the last year, but knowing how stingy management is. Maybe she'll be given a few Band-Aids and aspirin to hand out. A nurse is a good idea, but three shifts means we need three nurses.

Open House—The open house this week went well. But where was all the mist we choke on every day? If we want people to experience the real manufacturing plant. We should have run the machines and handed out respirators to the visitors.

Shift mis—information—The little dictator on second shift can't answer our questions at the monthly meetings. Why? Is it that he doesn't know any more than he's told? Why doesn't he get back to us. When he tells us he will, is he really stupid or is he acting that way?

Cry, cry baby—Every time someone asks Cry Baby Dog, in maintenance, can he have someone do some work. He jumps up and down and cries. I got one person hurt and six people out on vacation, blah blah blah blah blah blah . . .

Don't choke on it—It was national safety week, did anybody notice? Yeah, the company made a big deal out of it, passing out four lifesavers to each of us. That's really going to increase safety, now isn't it.

<u>Who's bright idea?</u>—Who's the brain who figured out to put the cafeteria smoking area right by the vending machines? Do they figure that only smokers use the vending machines? Or that non-smokers don't really mind smoke when they are getting something to eat.

<u>We might as well eat and smoke</u>—A while ago we were supposed to get a trade-off. The workers would give up eating and smoking on the grind lines and management would install a mist system and air conditioning. So what happened? The mist system doesn't seem to work at all. There is always a fog in here. It looks more like Los Angeles than clean-air and management never even turns on the air conditioner, it's always set at around 80°, sounds like we got the raw end of the deal.

<u>Cost savings</u>—The company wants big cost savings, they say. So why don't they get rid of Eachy Boy and ill-Pill? They can't make a decision without it Eachy, so just eliminate the middleman.

<u>Brain trouble</u>—Recently a person from first shift recently backed out from becoming a stupervisor. He cut his hair and everything getting ready for. It just goes to show you, the company ladder isn't always a step up. It's a good thing, he just lost his hair because he almost lost his mind!

<u>Volunteer? You're out to lunch!</u>—Geary is out to lunch, man forgot to post the shutdown schedule on time, by the time he posted it. Some of us have already made plans, and since it was late the schedule can't be mandatory. All he can do is ask for volunteers. Well,

have a good vacation, Geary. We know we will, when we're away from here!

<u>We need permanent changes</u>—The plant nurse told workers who are angry at the company to get counseling and that they need help. If all of us were treated like sugar and spice like the nurse is. We wouldn't be so angry or annoyed. The nurse might say, if you are being abused or angry. Go get some counseling to help understand your anger. We say <u>organize and fight</u> to change a system and the <u>reason</u> for the abuse.

<u>1984 and more!</u>—Looks like we might have a new time clock system using a card and a computer keeping track of our absenteeism. But with nine months of 100% production. Why spend all that money on a system to keep track of us more? Who's keeping track of them?

<u>Charity for chicken Little</u>—The Charity fund raiser is coming up. So get ready for a high pressure pitch from management. It's interesting that they care more about the Charity than they do about workers grievances. They'll even stop the line to collect your money. But if a worker has a problem. They'll act like the sky is falling if <u>you</u> stop the line.

<u>Why else</u>—If the nurse asks you why you need an aspirin, just tell her because this place gives me a <u>headache</u> ,that's why!

<u>Mystery sludge</u>—About a week ago all the drinking water in the plant was shut off and the cafeteria shut down. The drinking water was full of sludge, but if

management knows why they are not saying. For four days we were inconvenienced, and now all we know is that management says "all's well". The water may have cleared, but the mystery hasn't.

Long work means long rest—Personal days off are eight hours a day. Why? We work 12 hours a day! Where's our personal day over time?

Reject? What's the reject?—If anyone thinks our quality systems are good. Just look at final audit at the end of the month. Of course there is no problem at the beginning of the next month. They release it all!!

It doesn't add up—Lets see, the company will give us 11 uniforms and we will pay them to wash five uniforms a week. But a lot of us work seven days a week, and pretty soon we will be out of clean uniforms. There is a got to be a lot of dirty uniforms walking around this place.

Production Specialists?—We have heard that stupervisor blank blank will be going to the home for washed up stupervisors. He's got a new job with the company as an engineer, a so-called production specialist. Looks like the company takes care of its own. The company probably thinks that stupervisors are already production specialists, but they sure fooled us.

Plant slogan—Company/Union: A team dedicated to quality. Several ideas come to mind when we read this. Number one, it sounds more like a slogan written for the quality department. Number two, it must be a team without management. Number three, this slogan must be a goal, because that's not what's going on around here.

Believe it or not—The company should be in the Guiness book of world records. Being the only company still in business after centuries, and is still losing money. It's got to be a record. We think someone should call and report this truly unique annual event!

Just goes to show us—The company Hench boy fired a new hire because he was sleeping on the job. This person was working 12 hours a day seven days a week and working on day shift Sunday and he was to go to third shift Monday, which meant he would only have 8 hours between Sunday and Monday, shouldn't there be a break-in period? And another thing, we have seen this stupervisor's sleep with their eyes open for years!

The big D.—On day shift the stupervisor, DP, the Big D, tried to tell all the workers in the cafeteria to go back to work and leave the cafeteria, all this because we showed up one or two minutes early to our lengthy 20 minute lunch break. We think the Big D needs to take a chill pill!

Pizza—pizza—pizza—We get pizza today!, and that ain't no donut either! How often does someone get a free lunch? While we did do the work for it, but it would be nice if we got a big profit sharing checks to go along with our pizza. That must be too much to ask for!

Doomed from the start!—Banana Mite held shift meetings. He told us they were suspending morning meetings and wanted all machine operators to stay on their machines or lines until five minutes after the hour. This is supposed to help achieve 10 to 20,000 more bearings that day. We are to keep our machines running so the next shift coming in can continue to run them without any downtime between shifts. But even if we run our machines 15 minutes or more, and every shift does it, with even a five second cycle time for every line. Still, it's not enough!

"I'll take this write-up off your records as soon as I see a change in your attitude."

"I'm working smarter, not harder!"

"That's good! My attitude will change as soon as I walk out of your office."

"Someday, son, all of this can be yours!"

RULE NO. 104

"Ah -- it says right here in the Handbook, a win/win scenario means the company wins twice."

PASS THIS ON TO A FRIEND!

7 of 8

"It looks good around here with all the flowers and stuff. But there's very little shade since they took down the barbed-

<u>1% in February</u>—February is the month when we get our 1% bonuses. It sure would be nice for a change to get the money at the beginning of the month instead of the end. If this year is like the past. The Company will hold onto our money till the last second it can. The company <u>could</u> do us a favor this year, but don't look for it.

<u>New hires</u>—The company is doing some hiring so it has told hourly workers to turn in the names of friends and family who needed jobs. Of course, this gives management a chance to turn in the names of their friends and relatives to get hired. Let's all keep an eye on who they decide to choose.

<u>We don't want a crock</u>—Retiree health care is supposed to be an issue in this year's contract, and it is been said that it may cost us to get it written in our labor agreement. But why should it cost us anything at all? The company is already paying for it. So why would it cost us for something we already have? That <u>Turkey</u> won't fly! Were supposed to get something from the company. Instead of a longer-term warranty.

<u>Play the Eachy game</u>—To play, simply finished the following sentence and submitted it to the newsletter guy. Having Eachy in the plant is like . . . For example: "having Eachy in the plant is like having a cold sore on your first date" the possibilities are endless so play now and play often!

<u>Going to jail!</u>—Sam and Roger got taken out of the plant the other week, by uniform police officers, what were they charged with? Impersonating a stupervisor!, to bad it wasn't for real. They were taken in a cop car

to raise money for an hour for the fight against cancer and at the least, we got an hours worth of productive work out of them!

It's got to be a joke—What? The company is environmentally friendly? Ha, ha, ha. That's a big laugh! Must be a different company than the one we work for! The one we work for pollutes our air with kerosene mist with rust inhibitors and with carbon dust and with coolant oils. The only thing this is environmentally good for, is their bank account!

Win-win? But don't hold your breath—If the company is worried about the congestion in the plant parking lot. Why don't they stagger our starting times and quitting times. One third of the shift could start on the hour and leave on the hour. The next third could start at 5 minutes after the hour and leave 5 minutes after the hour and etc. That way we can get a paid lunch and a company gets less congestion in the parking lot, and it doesn't cost the company a penny!

Bearing component? No balls!—The company has no balls, or we mean is short of balls. No, that still doesn't sound right. Anyway, the company uses its balls so quickly they're always running out of ball components to assemble bearings. Why? The company has a ball plant in Kalamazoo?, can't they keep up with the amount of balls we need. Oh well, don't worry about it.

Oddball trash sniffer—Why did the engineer get so mad when he found some food wrappers in his trash can. He even went so far as to take the bag of trash over to play "show and tell" for the Quality Manager.

We have some questions for him?. Number one, what in the shop rules prevents us from putting trash in <u>your</u> trash can. Number two, is trash patrol a part of your new job now? Number three, are you mad because someone might have eaten something in the QA Lab. Number four, are you mad because you had to take out the garbage. Number five, do you sniff garbage at home and around your neighborhood? Also what other oddball hobbies do you have?

<u>First impressions are right</u>—Haven't you noticed when you're away for a while. Like a day or two, and you pull back into the parking lot. You get out of your car and start walking into the plant. When that company odor hits you, the kerosene and oil odors. Right there and then you know how much you haven't missed the whole place after all. That's enough to scare off man or beast, but of course only we could know that's nothing compared to working inside!

<u>Improving his lot</u>—Ronnie has come back home to the Union. He might owe for May's union dues. But just think. He doesn't have to take the company's crap anymore. Even working in heat treat department looks better than stupervision.

<u>Mind your own business</u>—Someone was suspended a few weeks ago for going to a bar. The person was out on a medical leave for their back and the company says, that means you can't go to a bar! Why? When did it become a illegal to drink a beer? And what has your back got to do with drinking a beer? Management should spend less time trying to run our personal lives and more time addressing problems in the plant. Like

the oil mist in the air, that people have to breathe every day.

A history lesson—remember when :
> . . . we had a profit sharing plan?
> . . . we had Good Friday off?
> . . . we had a horseshoe pit out back?
> . . . we could smoke in the plant?
> . . . we could go out to eat lunch?

The good quit early!—The personnel secretary Lorna, wrote in her letter to the plant workers before she quit. The success of the company doesn't only lie in the hands of people at the top. It belongs to you, without you making the product no one else would have a job. We would like to add to that, Lorna. We could do it without the people at the top! The workers are the bearings that hold this factory together and make it run.

A few good days—Memorial day weekend was great. We had some time to do the things we like to do. But on Tuesday, we were back at the plant thinking about the next time we get a few days off.

A Bright idea!—Why is it so dark in the storage component area? We need light to read labels. And people are running hi-lows and moving in and out of that area..People are going in and out of the office all day walking by. So why not light it up like the rest of the plant? Maybe management could squeeze a little money out of their big bonus checks for a little more light!

History lesson, part two—remember when??? Ill Ill-Pill was the union chairman and took us out on strike.
Big Scary fired about a third of management in the plant.
And top management fired a string of personnel managers.
Chucky Please lost his bid for a new absentee policy.

Where is the communication?—We're being told, everything is looking beautiful in the contract negotiations. No problems, don't worry, everything will turn out just fine. It sounds like lambs being taken to slaughter to us.

Plant manager—Well, welcome back. Were all wondering how you are going to manage the plant. Are you going to follow the "company boys" style or are you going to be like Elvis and manage like a hermit, are you bringing people, like Batman brought Chucky Please. Were hoping you'll be fair, with all your dealings with us. Were hoping you will care more about the people than work, than production or the machines. But time will tell!

Their pockets have holes in them—There is a hole in the roof, and it's leaking all over the floor. This is a safety problem. And in the right conditions, someone walking on a wet floor by machines with 440 electricity could get electrocuted. What happened to all the money to repair the roof? You would think with all these new machines there would still be money left over to patch the roof. Did Elvis take it with him? Or did they give it to all the foremen for a bonus?

<u>More power to us</u>—Seems an employee was written up for a category "B" offense . . . loitering, horseplay and wasting company time. Can we do the same to the stupervisors with the "modern operating agreement"?

<u>On leave, full-time</u>—Chucky Please said in his letter to us additional information will be required for the continuation of medical restrictions, on hours worked. But it looks like the same old shit to us! It looks like they don't trust our doctors anymore either. Top management doesn't need restrictions on hours. They only work part time anyway!

<u>The doghouse</u>—Third shift set up a doghouse for a stupervisor who is known as Dawg. He should learn how to behave if he doesn't want to be in the doghouse. And let the other stupervisors beware, or they might end up in the doghouse too!

<u>Blue phone, please</u>—A new supervisor on day shift got an initiation last week. He picked up a phone with machine blueing on it. You really have to be careful with those phones!

<u>Pearly whites for 30%</u>—Our new dental plan pays 100% of cleaning and 70% of regular tooth repair. It's been long overdue. It isn't the best plan, but it's better than nothing. Were guessing, but it probably cost less than Blue Cross Blue Shield for better coverage. And that's why the company went for it. In other words, it's not because they care that much about us and our families, pearly whites.

Nurse alert—The nurse has been at it again, she argues with everyone and their doctors about whether they really are injured. She acts like she doesn't believe what everyone is really injured. Maybe she was trained by the plant manager. Maybe she's been moved to personnel without telling anyone. We were wondering what her new title should be. She's not acting like a nurse, if anyone has an idea what she should be called let the news letter people know.

Recipe for stress—It's funny, the company wants us to exercise and to keep our stress levels down. But they won't lower the alarm in assembly. It sounds like a police car in the middle of the assembly room, with its siren on! Yes, this is a great stress reducer!

Can he take a hint?—From the did you know Department. September was a historic day for the company Ill-Pill's 30 year anniversary. You can retire after 30 years, right?

Black chairs, lower stress—New chairs in conference room 15. This must be so when they write us up for the new absentee and blameless absentee policy. We remain comfortable.

Lost in a dream—Eachy must think by dreaming up those new charts about the scrap in color. It will help him save his job, well keep on dreaming!!!

Sweeping it under the rug—We never heard anything about how the inventory turned out. We shut down production all weekend and they scheduled, [made] half of us take inventory and then tell us nothing. Inventory couldn't have gone well. We didn't hear a lot of bragging from them!

Put them where the sun don't shine—Personnel has finally done it. They have given out the absentee %'s, but they have figured them based on 40 hours a week and made all kinds of mistakes on the days we took off. It only goes to show you, they make the rules we have to go by, but they can't even keep track of us all, ha, ha !!

Three jobs—When we got hired here. We each signed on for one job. So why are we working two and three jobs now in some areas one person is expected to work on three machines. This shouldn't be a problem for those of us with three pairs of arms!

Two policies, one company—Does management work for the company like we do? If they do, how come they don't have the same "your fault" absentee policy that we do? Maybe it's because it doesn't affect their work when they don't show up.

No prevailing rate—An electrician quit and went to work for one of the big three for much more money. It's funny, a person's wages are based on the company you work for, not the type of job we do, but the price we pay for a gallon of milk or a TV or gas for our cars stays the same. If prices were based on our ability to pay, the rich would pay the highest prices and some wouldn't have to pay all.

November elections—There is an election coming up in November, every election the politicians say the same thing "vote for me and I'll set you free", and then they turn around and attack us once they are elected. The truth is that any rights we have or gains that we have made. We have won through struggle, the politicians are busy defending the interests of their rich friends. We can only depend on ourselves to defend our own interests!

Why not other charities?—Everyone we know couldn't wait to give to the X charities. We want to keep the Concorde jet full of fuel so top executives can fly to France or anywhere for that matter. At the drop of a hat. And of course we want to give, so that they can hire more office help to make themselves look important and their meager salaries? Only over a couple of hundred thousand per year. Of course we want to give all we can to that . . . not!!

Set your sights high—Wow, look at all the salaried jobs posted up six so far this year, and you could guess how many hourly jobs have been posted. Right, zero. So much for the plant managers, cutting back on salary hiring. No wonder they're losing big money. He needs to hire more workers to make bearings. That's really where the money comes from.

Price drop—Vending prices on the machines came down. Coffee is now 10 cents a cup less.10 cents a cup really adds up for people who drink 3 cups a day and work seven days a week. That's over $100 a year.

Good news—At the last plant wide meeting a couple weeks ago. The plant manager talked about how things are really looking good, we'll Mr. Plant manager ,we are really happy for you. But when are we going to get some good news?

Same old story—At that same meeting, we found out that the company didn't make any money. That's at least five years in a row that this company hasn't made a dime, were told. That must mean that there is no money for new machinery or high salaries for management. Maybe we should take up a collection, . . . not!

No problem—Yes we have quality problems in our plant, but think of it in a positive light. We don't see any reject tickets until the parts are stacked up on pallets and are ready to be shipped out. Eachy must be doing something right!!

When you're young and have a life—When new-b's get their time in the Union and in six months they start missing time. But why? It couldn't be too much over time, no it couldn't be, there only working 56 to 82 hours a week. That won't affect someone that young, the company is all there is in life, right? Wrong! The union should stand beside us if we miss a couple of days right? Why, their for a shorter workday? With the same amount of pay, right? So how could the company fire someone for missing time, when they get every weekend and off.

Absentee policy—Over Memorial Day, we were thinking about management's absentee policy. We understand that there are not big problems if they miss work, but still we think we should have the same absentee policy they have. This would allow us to have some time off, and see our families and enjoy life a little more.

Good for all or bad for all—When we go on a new job. The company makes us work for lower wages, called

Charlie Reed

training pay. Why not training pay for the stupervisors when there reassigned.

Big brother—Drugs and alcohol in the plant? The company always uses it as an excuse to look in our lockers and our toolboxes. And since they don't have anything better to do, maybe there taking the time to listen in on us while we talk on the phone's.

Cancer—Cancer and the company, how they seem to go together. There have been too many people getting cancer that have worked here. Some chemicals that cause cancer have been eliminated from the workplace. But many have not even been studied, do they cause cancer? We don't even know. And since cancer takes time to develop, exposure over years could be the reason, someone develops cancer. We should have a cancer study to help determine how much a risk there is to work here and to tell us how to better our chances to survive working at the company all of our lives.

New plant slogan—Cracked in America, Rejected round the world!!

The best way is the worker's way—Workers were told to take off stickers from our toolbox's that management deems as provocative and trouble-making language. Japanese bashing and racism are wrong. And we know it, but leave our toolbox's alone. Management tells us we must do things the "Japanese way", but it looks like the "American way". All we see is the "stupervisor's way". So, stop telling us it's the "Japanese way" and start telling us. It's "management's way". Stop blaming the Japanese for everything you do.

Harassment is no romance—This definition of sexual-harassment was submitted by a worker to the company and we thought you would like it. We do. "Sexual-harassment has much less to do with Sex than with power. It is the way in which one person illegitimately, coercively exercises power over another, usually men over women, although there are other combinations. It is designed to discriminate, to intimidate and to dehumanize. It refuses to take no for an answer, far from romance. It is hostile and offensive". Spot on !!

Hidden eggs?—At the company, toolmakers have always done some strange things in the past. It has always been said that Dimwity is always a day late and a dollar short. But whoever heard of an Easter egg hunt in October? What were you looking for the Easter Bunny?

Nothing in the socks, but odor—At the company we have a new president, has it made a big difference to workers? No. It's a lot of the same old crap over again. It just goes to show you. You can change the feet, but the socks still stink, and he might even smell bad to, but we haven't seen him enough to know that.

Management type—The company has its own Loser air head. She blames others for her mistakes. Even tries to manage the department from home. She pays so much attention to others that she doesn't do her own job.

Job un-fair—The local newspaper keeps showing us how bright and cheery our job prospects are. On September 17, they reported about the many opportunities at the local mall. The mall had a job fair to fill a bunch of low paid clerks jobs for all the dinky little shops. The mall bosses were very generous. There was no charge for filling out the applications at the fair.

The beastly baby—Have you ever seen a little baby whose an absolute beast? That whenever she misses her nap she starts screaming and crying at anything. We've got one at the company, but she's a stupervisor in assembly! She'll start bawling if feeding time comes just a minute or two late. She even threw a tantrum at the Quality big-wig the other day. Somebody give the beast a pacifier and put her down for a nap!

Something to remember—A woman at the company had her house burn down. She was given a fresh-start party, which coworkers showered her with presents. This shows how workers can organize to take care of each other. Anyone who says we stand alone is just plain wrong!

Step up to the challenge—The personnel department at the company wrote a letter to a worker in the G4 department, which said you have been ordered to climb on machines to make adjustments and clear up hangups. The company shop rule book states never climb on machines, common sense and their rule book are correct. It is unsafe to climb on the machines, but if they want us to climb on machines we will, right after we shut them off!

How bright can you get?—The local newspaper told us on Monday that the area jobs seekers should see good hiring prospects. Gee., where are all the jobs hiding? In temporary work? The survey was done by manpower to see how much big bucks they can make by paying hungry people peanuts. No problem making house payments with that.

Company news flash—Worker back on the job after being terminated more than seven months. Arbitrator ruled in unions favor, but with no back pay, chalk one up for us!

Take care of the real problems—OSHA, conducted and on-sight inspection at the company last week and observed many problems throughout the plant. The biggest single problem, the personnel department chose to get all excited about was safety glasses. Why? To divert our attention from the real problem, management?

You can stop the harassment now!—Management has been harassing workers about their workers-comp cases. The personnel manager wants to reduce the amount of workers now claiming workers comp. That's stupid, they are the ones injured because of all the speedups, repetitive motion jobs and slippery floors in the plant. The company is responsible for those injuries, and they should pay!

Kneel-down is trying—At the plant kneel-down has been doing much better lately. He's only pissed off only half of the plant and thrown out only a few dozen chairs or so and written up only a few of us.

Employee involvement—At the company, the extent of employee involvement so far has been to explain the company policy. Employee involvement to us means one worker ties the foreman up, while another worker chooses the type of pie to throw, handing the pie to another worker. So he can throw it in the foremans face. That's teamwork at its best!

Do onto others—Workers at the company finally got our new contract books. Gee, not bad. It's only been nine months since the contract was ratified. Funny thing . . . management takes all this time to print up the contract books and pass them out. But they don't abide by it anyway. That can go both ways, if they don't feel bound to the contract. We can ignore some of the rules also.

Strange noises—The floor managers at the company have been acting very strange lately. They've been imitating the sound of a whip while walking the shop floor. We ain't no beasts of burden! But if they think a little sound will make a difference in what we do, we've got our own answer: We could imitate a fire alarm and take an extra break, when we evacuate the building!

Missing in action—The company took an inventory recently, one of many lately. They didn't say but we wonder if they're still looking for those missing components. Just a few you know, only $1,700,000 worth !

What law?—The company is openly breaking the law, while the male workers get a morning and afternoon break plus lunch, women workers only get the morning break plus lunch. We're learning that workers rights are enforced only when we enforce them ourselves. Maybe that 80% that showed up for the last union meeting will tell the company's something.

Thanks—Thank you to all those who donated to the newsletter. Your contributions make it possible for the newsletter to keep coming out. Newsletter contributors know: If workers want something done. We can't rely on anyone else. We've got to do it ourselves!

Duck imitations—Management got a good picture of what the workers think of the job they've done this year. When the company picnic rolled around, only 30 people signed up to go. Or maybe the workers are just smart. On the day of the picnic, it rained and rained and the managers and stupervisors got to go for a swim. Too bad they don't know enough to come out of the rain!

More than one way to kill a rat—Kneel-down hopes to get a raise every time he appears in the newsletter. That's funny because we do to, maybe if he gets too many raises. They will fire him for being too costly or maybe he will quit because his head is all swelled up.

Fools looking for fool's—The company spent $190,000 on recruiting salary workers in the 1990s. That is more than we got in profit sharing in the last two years we got it. Now, sourly workers have been told to take two days off without pay and all hourly workers will get at least one week lay off. All that money and look at what they got for it. Do we have to say more?

Millage, thumbs down—County voters turned down a recent millage vote that would have provided money for an unemployment training program by two to one. Not that we don't need worker training programs and jobs, but they came to the wrong people for the money.

We pay enough in taxes as it is. We were given only two options higher taxes or no programs, but there is another option. It's the companies that get the trained workers, so make the companies pay for it

OSHA . . . for company profits—The Dayton Ohio daily news recently ran a series of reports showing that OSHA is not protecting workers among other things, the newspaper found in 20 years only one employer had been sent to jail for violating OSHA safety standards. Employers rarely paid large fines, even when they're found at fault for accidents. One company paid only two dollars for causing the deaths of two workers!. Some senators say they don't like these findings. So what are they proposing? To study the problem further. The senators said that OSHA ought to wear a sign saying, for shame",but that doesn't even come close. OSHA and Congress should wear a sign saying "for company profits" and the signs would be written in blood.

News bulletin—Does everybody know that a certain quality manager spends most of her day bs'ing with friends. Hey, we have some pictures to look at too!

Shut-in stupervisors—The week before last, we had no stupervisor in G6 for the last couple of days. You would be surprised how well the department ran. Production was up, morale was up. We don't need those bosses, they would be better off to pay them to stay home!

There is cooler air somewhere—How about this heat! For those of us in the plant. It's even hotter here than it is outside. Time for a picnic in the front offices!

Production percentages—Each day a % is mentioned at the departmental meetings. How come nothing is being said about the hidden cost of the extra dead weight in the salary department waiting for as long as two years to go to another plant.. Why aren't these people laid off until they are needed in two years, and the company wants cost savings?

Why is that?—Why is it that the front office personnel leave before the afternoon shift arrives? And don't arrive until midnight shift is long gone?

Safety last—Why does it seem that most of the evacuation routes, the aisles throughout the plant are always blocked?

Holiday . . . not—Why would management schedule us to work over the holiday weekend, if they really cared about us and our families?

Summer shutdown—Why does it take so long, every year to get a work schedule for summer shutdown made? We do have lives, you know!

It doesn't add up—Why is it that counting every piece of scrap is so important when management does not get the accurate account of what is coming in at the door? Who knows how many pieces are vendors short us every day instead are counted against us as lost or scrap parts and management turns around and counts this against our production bonus.

Ill Pills, bedtime story!—Someone forgot to inform Ill Pill, new-b's don't go on jobs that haven't been posted yet, is Ill- Pill asleep or what?

Jim Beam's worried about our safety glasses. We're worried about his prescription!

"I mean, why not up production? We don't have to work the 12-hours!!"

JELLY BONUS

"I'd like to deposit my bonus, please..."

"Does this mean he can't work 4 over tomorrow?"

"Golly, you have been so good to us this year, running all that production and all. We want to give you a x-mas gift this year. We're going to actually honor the labor agreement for the month of January!"

"Wow! Now we know how you got your name! ILL BILL."

Think about the people—We received two letters on how three union officials are having a good time running on all the union trips . . . . It's that time again. Our union dollars are hard at work. Our President, vice president and secretary all went to California to a convention. Only thing is they took their wives, so they can make a vacation out of it like the last time. They say it's costing between 10 and $15,000. No wonder we can't get a new union hall seems as though our president has everyone wrapped so they'll do anything he wants. Our union dollars are paying for hotel rooms, food, tickets and whatever else they want. Hey guys hope you had a good time, may be our next president will think about the people instead of himself . . . . No wonder we have to work so much over time, the union guys are never on their jobs, too busy being company or just sitting in their office making plans to spend our money.

Friendly or unfriendly—We heard the company was environmentally friendly.? What about all of the oily gloves that are thrown into the trash daily ? And the grease barrel liners? And all the pads used to soak up small oil spills? And what about all the grease thrown into the trash barrels daily when we clear the air from grease lines?

Vacation—Why do we have to be one of the plants where the employees are forced to take their vacations when management wants us to?

Back to his old tricks—Old PG is back. He only had to be good for a second. But now it's back to messing up things again today and tomorrow. Hey, look here. It's PG, the closest thing to a horse's tail!

<u>Down boy down!</u>—The dog is digging himself another hole. He's barking at everyone he sees. That kind of dog is the reason we are getting the MOA. Dog gone the dirty dog gone.

<u>It's a blue day</u>!—Who puts blueing on phones? Who gets blued? And who doesn't? It's up in the air or should we say, it's on the phones. For the pranksters, it's funny, and we mean funny, but for the poor souls who has to clean it off their ears. It's not funny at all. We think blueing is meant for management, all the others beware!

<u>Profit without MOA</u>—The company made a profit of .531 million last year. But was it because of the MOA . . . no. The MOA could be good for us if we can use it to improve our day-to-day life around the plant. But if all the company is going to do is to cut jobs. Then we don't need it, because the company did too much of that before it.

<u>Fair is fair</u>—On second and third shifts people in P5 were scheduled for 12 hours. But on first shift, it was voluntary for 10 hours a day. Why is the difference? It seems like the fair thing would be to offer the same deal to every one.

<u>That old game</u>—The roll process and automatic screw machines that they are talking about moving out of the plant, were paid for with the wealth of our work provided. We have a right to those jobs. And the workers at the other plant are in the same situation they have a right to jobs too. The company would like to see us and the workers at the other plant compete against each other. Then, the company wins. And we

lose. But when we workers stick together, we increased our numbers and strengthen our fight.

Missed the loop—The dog has gone around and told us the MOA he will never work. The MOA won't work with stupervisors like him. The dog is out of his yard and out of the loop!

Mercy!—It's crazy!!! . . . Ill Pills promoted . . . PG's is releasing all the rejects . . . new stupervisors hired right before MOA . . . customers complaining about no grease . . . profit sharing a little too little, a lot too late . . . Where are we going and does it have a name!

Contract?—It's been almost 9 months since we voted on the contract, and we still haven't seen it. Maybe they haven't finished writing it yet.

A pat on the back—Big scary sent Pat to work in plant personnel. Why? We believe it was to find out what is going on. Seems she really took care of the problems. Keep up the good work Pat !

Confused—It seems the Rubber-head is baffled by what so many people have, and still want to come back to the shop floor. Gee, maybe he should ask the ones that have driven them back. That is the Rock-head boys.

Rubber stampers—It didn't take long for Rubber-head to start running with the wrong crowd. The stoned-head boys have done nothing for the plant except run it down. So when rubber head came along, the stoned-head boys didn't know if they could incorporate rubber-head into the crowd as a power base. The transformation has been fairly complete now. Now they're all running around the plant like they're solving problems, but it's only smoke and mirrors.

Job opening—Ill Pill will be retiring soon. With this comes his replacement and a new stupervisor and both from the other plant. How were these replacements decided on? These jobs could be opened up to people from this plant too. Or did they have someone already in mind? Once again, it's not what you know, it's who you know.

Looking for quality?—Some one-inch bearings should have been hardened, but we produce them with soft ends for a year or two, may be more. Why? Why don't you ask trashman? Maybe he was so busy looking in the trash cans he didn't have time to do his job!

Gone . . . gone . . . gone . . . —Cheesehead has left us. Of course, we are real sad about this. Maybe we should have a going away party. Now that he's gone!

Broken records—We made records for production twice in the recent past. The first time we got a free Subway sandwich. Then we went further and broke that record right away. Well, management showed us all how to act. They didn't go any further the second time and brought in just the subs again.

Saving our ship—It's good to see the company so involved and "environmentally friendly" to help save our environment. All the trees cut down to make all those pallets will grow back in 30 or 40 years, maybe. And just think all those pallets they grind up. They aren't oil soaked or anything. So when they put them in and on the ground as mulch around other trees and shrubs. Why, you know, they will grow better. And of course we all know underground water is much better with a little company oil and grease mixed in. And if you think something doesn't sound right. Your right, this only happens in the company's fairy tales!

Rested and ready—Must be nice, the top managers looked so relaxed and rested. It must be all those weekends off, and the light workloads they have. If we didn't know any better. We'd think they didn't work at all. But we know better. We've seen them picking lint off their chairs as they are sitting at their desks!

Flexible schedule—Management has been more flexible about overtime lately. People have choices, whether or not to take it working 10 hours rather than 12. This matches their needs right now. But what about our needs? Shouldn't the schedule match our needs, too.

Important information—The survey results were very useful. One of the questions was, how can we communicate better? And the answer was being more effective communicators. Thanks for the information, we'll work on that.

Rose-colored glasses—We heard one of the members of the MOA committee was asking around about why the survey results were so negative. If she was really concerned about the results. All she had to do was read the companies report on the survey. Nothing negative there!

Charlie Reed

Are you listening?—The survey results don't look much like anything we said. They looked like they had the results even before they had the survey handed out to us. What's the point of doing this survey then? It just goes to show you the workers didn't need the MOA, management did

Where is this leading us—Don't be misled by all the little junior executives who say the MOA will solve everyone's problems. Management wants the MOA to lead to speedups, increased workloads, and as a result to an unsafe work environment. All in the name of profits. What has management done so far with all the profits? Bought more machines to run more bearings, with less workers. We can run 100,000 bearings a day, when we use to run that many in a month. Has this helped us to lower our workloads?

How long?—A couple of our fellow workers had their fingers torn off by the machines they were working on. Why do we stand around and do nothing when this happens? We go right on with blood and skin on the machines. Like oh well, we might as well accept it, who will be the next? You . . . me? How long will this go on? Until enough is enough? How many of us carry scars around with us on our fingers, hands and arms? How many more will have to be hurt before we say, we're not going to take it any longer!

Faster . . . faster . . . faster . . . —Will assembly, have to start to put unassembled bearings in the boxes. Just to get the parts out? That's about as fast as we can go!

Hot seat—Ill Pill is on the hot seat again over race discrimination. We bet that before it's over, he will be able to sit on some machine stock and heat treat it.

Which is worse?—Is there anything free? The flu shots were or were they? And a lot of people who got the flu shots also got the flu symptoms. And some were off work one or two, and even more days because of it. So why would the company knowingly give us something to make us miss more work? Also, would the company be truthful about how many people missed work since having the flu shot? We don't know, but some drug company recommended that everyone get a flu shot of their drug. So it must be good for us. And of course this is just the reaction of all people to the flu shot to get the symptoms of a flu. So which is worse, the symptoms or the flu?

Absentee percentage—Why was it at the ratification meeting, they didn't tell us the formula for absentee percentage? Gee. Wonder why?

Remember when . . . —
#1 The company recommended we get the swine flu shots?
#2 Big scary fired all those stupervisors, and how good we felt?
#3 We had a horseshoe pit out back and played on our lunches?
#4 The company told us to work smarter, not harder?
#5 We had a hot lunch on second shift too?

The Left Hook :
Part two

CB

Truth in advertising—Have you noticed all these campaign ads lately. It's kind of funny, each one is accusing his opponent of being a liar, a cheat and a puppet of big business. But the joke is there all right!

Company business—The company has tried twice to get us workers to accept losses and twice the workers voted the contract proposal down. These were contracts that the bargaining committee endorsed. This raises the question, is the union all the workers or is it a few people sitting at a table? It's up to the workers to choose a contract. And it's up to the workers to decide when to fight. And when they're ready to fight, the workers deserve a leadership that is ready to work with them, not against them.

Rumor mill—At the company the plant manager has told everyone not to talk to Cheesy Peter the big cheese in sales and distribution. He's been canned, effective August 1. The plant manager says talking to cheesy, might affect legislation involving "our" tax status. Are we supposed to care? He also says no one has been convicted of a crime yet but law enforcement agents are currently involved in the matter. So stay

Charlie Reed

away from cheesy, we might learn about the cheesy deals they are all into. The rumor mill might be turned into a grinding mill for the plant manager!

<u>Workers refused bad contract</u>—Ill-Pill has failed twice in his attempts to have workers approve the bad deals he works out with his buddies at the top. Last Friday, workers voted down the crumbs that dropped off of the company's table. When we come to work, we will want to make a living, not pay for our own benefits. How many more times will we have to turn down the contract before the company gets the message. As many times as it takes, that's how many!

<u>Adventures in dreamland</u>—The company just instituted a new absentee policy that wasn't mentioned anywhere in the contract. What is it? We voted on our contract, but we never had a chance to vote on this!. Why are they afraid to let everyone decide on this. Why should we have it dictated to us? We know what's best for us, heck we run this place every day. Management just sits up in their offices, dreaming up absentee policies that are unworkable. Hey, somebody wake those dreamers up, will ya !?

<u>Million Dollar baby</u>—The company just spent millions on a new carburizing furnace. The funny thing is, why won't it run production yet? The case depth of the parts isn't right, and they have it on a 60 minute cycle. The old carb ran a 20 minute cycles, which is three times faster than the new carb. Great investment huh? But we workers will take it, we'd rather work three times slower any day.

62

Vending machine ripoff—Contract time for workers is a time when companies try and get part of our wallets. Ever notice the vending machine companies do the same around contract time. Seems like every time we get a wage increase. They raise the prices five or 10 cents, ever buy at 50 cent apple. That's equal to over $100 a bushel, companies should be providing vending machine service to us at cost. Why should everyone profit from everything we do? It's not like we're going to the movies!

Money for workers too?—All workers are being offered 12 hours a day. You work eight hours on your regular job and if you want to, you can work four hours overtime to sort parts. Quality problems are mounting in the plant and rejected parts are stacking up. We have the Japanese quality systems in the plant. The best in the world, and we still have quality problems. If management really didn't want rejected parts, why hasn't management listened to us, the workers? But management doesn't care. We tell them about the problem, and they say, no problem will well sort them at the end of line. They are in too big a hurry running production, and we get "zero defects" through sorting. Will the company write the check for our new contract coming up out of the same checkbook used to write the check for sorting parts? We hope so.

Gas pains in the?—The first thing you heard about the Iraqi invasion was how gas prices would go up. The third day after . . . some pumps were up 7 to 14cents. It's a fast tanker to get that more expensive oil here in only three days and refine it to boot. Oil companies will hide behind the Iraqi war to rip us off. Just like the last oil crisis, if their cost goes up a cent. They will charge us a dime, and then blame somebody 10,000 miles away.

63

"Ah -- it says right here in the
Handbook, a win/win scenario means the
company wins twice."

Are you listening Guinness?—The plant manager holds small group meetings with about 10 workers at a time every month or so. It is doubtful if anything of benefit to the workers will come out of these meetings. There was one reported comment by a worker that was noteworthy, though. The plant manager was told "this place should be in the Guinness world book of records". "It has the biggest collection of bigots, idiots, liars and thieves in the world of supervision".

Major mistake—A while back there was a real foul-up at the company, a lot of bad parts were put out and of course workers were blamed for it. But how often have parts that were tagged rejects been removed by a foreman, who said "that's okay, let it pass". What's the use of having a foreman if he can't catch mistakes in his department?

What big hearts, they have—Well, the Company executives decided to cancel their big hotel dinner for all employees. Guess they were even smart enough to figure out that a dinner for all employees is silly. When most employees won't be coming anyway. Instead the bosses decided to have a steak fry for all workers in the plant for lunch one day in the plant cafeteria. Wow, how about that. 15 years in and you get a free lunch!

An alarming trend—Workers at the company have noticed an alarming trend. This past year three or four workers have died of cancer. Just a couple years ago, several more workers were cancer victims. How many more have to die before the company decides to do something about this? The company says they don't have the ability to look into something like that. But just recently, they called in experts from the university to figure out why so many workers were coming down with contact dermatitis. Of course a lot of workers had to start complaining before they did something about it. This is what they need to do now and figure out what in this plant is killing us and get some results quick!

Do as I say, not as I do—The company is planning on having a big dinner at the hotel to award all employees for their service with the company. But why are the corporate office employees the "Taj Mahal" having their own dinner on a different day. The dinner is supposedly to award all employees, but if you have less than five years. You can't come, if you have less than 15 years. You can bring your spouse, but if you are a department head or a plant manager and have less than five years. It's okay, you can still come to the dinner, and to no one's surprise, there will be plenty of seating and food but there will still be one thing clearly missing employees!

Why ask, you may not like the answer—A supervisor asked a worker while on break why he was laughing, afterwards, the supervisor went to personnel to complain that the worker used dirty words in a threatening way. And wouldn't you know it. The worker got three days off, well, I guess he can take the pay loss, but "virgin ears" won't be the same again!

The turkeys are shooting—The new no-fault absentee policy at the plant is a joke. The policy will allow no doctors excuses if you get sick. You have to use one of your personal days, and you can be fired after only 30 hours of un-excused absences. After they tell us they're not accepting excuses. If this is really no-fault, then no one should be blamed for absences, but surprise, managements policy just means <u>they</u> don't get blamed. Management treats their job like a turkey shoot. How many can they shoot down between hiring and retirement? But now, who gave the turkeys guns?

<u>The 3 o'clock meetings</u>—Management has devised a "humane way" to lay people off. They told people one day were going to have a meeting at 3 p.m.. You'll find out what it's all about then, by 3:30 they were out on the street. don't like it? They've got a 3 p.m. meeting for you too. Do they think they've got a "lock" on meetings. Well, the workers could very easily have their own 3:00 clock meeting!

<u>Emperors new clothes</u>—Management at the plant is seeing things. They have a habit of accusing workers of wrongdoing without evidence. They'll pull out phantom witnesses who disappear when a worker tries to see them. Like the Emperor's new clothes, but they swear they saw a witness. Right after they saw the tooth fairy!

<u>Rude awakening</u>—Management at the plant just learned a lesson, the rest of us learned a long time ago. A lot of people who were recently laid off came from management. People with 20 years were tossed out on their buts, management people sometimes think just because they wear a white shirt. Sit behind a desk and do the companies bidding, their jobs are more secure than ours. In reality, they are no different from us. Their just as disposable when the company wants to make more profit. Kind of says something

doesn't it, pick your allies carefully or you'll be getting a rude awakening.

They've got it backwards—Management is all upset because production has been down the last couple of months. Management blames the workers, of course, they tell us we're not working hard enough. They expect us to feel guilty about it, but were not that stupid, responsibility lies with management. Everyone knows that scheduling has been crazy lately. Not to mention that our jobs are so overloaded. It's impossible to keep up with them. If management wants to put pressure on someone they ought to put pressure on themselves to stop screwing up our work.

Reality check—At the plant our bosses act like they can tell us to do what ever, they act like they can get away with anything. And they'd like us to believe it. They think, they are more important than we are, but if the white shirts disappeared, would the work place fall apart? No way. We'd run it better by ourselves. But if we stopped working, what would happen? A lot of white shirts would be flying around like chickens with their heads cut off, and they'd be just as effective.

Training and indoctrination—The plant manager announced that a new plant manager will take his place later this year. Meanwhile, the new guy will be spending his time training with a few workers in different departments, and this has never been done before. The plant manager calls this a "training and indoctrination". Well, we'll make sure he's indoctrinated real well!

Great fertilizer—At the company we just had our benefits replaced with crap. They sure didn't open their chests and let their hearts fall out. Of course, the company talks about how good their packages are but in reality the only thing it's good for, is fertilizing our gardens.

Call the cops!—We workers at the company have a lot in common with other workers these days. We get paid so low it's hard to even live, let alone raise a family the way the company pays us is outright robbery. Somebody call the cops and report a theft!

No reason to kill ourselves—Management is slowly tightening the screws on workers with there speedups. Every day it's a little more pressure to work harder, doing more in less time. It's gotten to the point where one person working at an average speed can only hope to finish 80% of a work. Management has simply made these jobs bigger than we can do. There is no way we can get it all done. Heck, we might as well take some time to sit back and take a rest. And let more work go by, won't hurt us any.

Big scary's latest joke—The company just opened its newly renovated heat treat facilities last week at the dedication ceremonies last Monday. Big scary told us all, that the dedication was another example of the company's commitment to its employees in the area. Commitment to the employees? Big Scary must be a comedian. A decade ago, this plant employed over 400 workers. Now were down to around 200, all these laid-off workers sure found out about the company's commitment. But only to corporate greed, not employee need. Workers call him Big Scary because his nose grows every time he opens his mouth.

<u>Peace dividend savings at work?</u>—We've been hearing a lot about the peace dividend lately. How the end of the Cold War will create money when the government cuts the defense budget. But now Congress and the president are talking about raising our taxes!. What are they doing with all that money? Building monuments for the presidents.

<u>To many hurt and killed workers</u>—April 28 is Workers Memorial Day, a day to remember the workers killed on the job this year. Injuries and deaths on the job are a serious problem. One of every four workers is hurt on the job, each year. The speedups mean that many more workers are injured or sick and damaged by their jobs. For the bosses this is just a minor inconvenience for higher profits, but it is a cost that the workers cannot afford to pay with their lives and our health. We don't need to sacrifice that to make the rich wealthier. Stop the speedups, the damage and the deaths.

<u>Who deserves to be fired?</u>—It's crazy when workers get fired for alcoholic abuse. Certainly alcoholism is a problem especially for the worker who suffers from it and it needs to be addressed. But how does firing someone address the problem? It doesn't. It just gets it out of the company's hair. If someone is to be fired for abuse, we should be able to fire management for abusing <u>us</u>.

<u>Crybabies</u>—Ever since the company moved the plant to a new location, the company thinks it can do whatever it wants with us. They act like the workers

owe the company for getting us out of the hell hole we were working in before. They act like they've made a big sacrifice for us. You can just hear them whining: oh, the taxes are too high. Oh, the bills are too high. Oh, boo-hoo boo-hoo, somebody give the babies a bottle and put them to bed!

Employee assistance?—Does your company have an employee assistance program? Better watch out. It just might assist you right out of your job.

Pure baloney—They've been putting the screws on the workers lately. Up till recently we've been working 12 hour shifts with no lunch breaks. Even now, were working nine hours shifts with no lunches. You can bet that management takes a lunch. How many good parts, do they really think are going out between 12 and 1 pm. If they don't watch out, there going to find parts made with sandwich meat soon.

What's the real problem?—We keep hearing how the Japanese are the cause of our problems. The government, the media and the corporations keep telling us it's the Americans against the Japanese. But the Japanese workers aren't the problem. They've got the same kind of problems we do. Japanese corporations are trying to do the same thing as American corporations right here. Make the biggest profit they can off backs of the workers. In Japan or in the US, the problem for workers is the same thing . . . the corporations!!

And they say it's safe?—A lot of us are on jobs, where we use chemicals every day. Our eyes burn, our hands breakout and we leave with a bad taste in our mouths every day. We can read the labels that say these chemicals are no good for us. But we still have to work with this stuff. OSHA always says this stuff is safe, no matter what it is. But our bodies tell us it's not safe. Do they expect us to believe them or our bodies?

The black hole—What the heck is the city doing with our money? Our roads are just as bad as any other city, are garbage pickup is just as bad. So are the rest of our services and our taxes are out of sight too.. All of these high tech businesses moving in and getting the benefit of our money. But we can be proud. We have the most expensive potholes in the state. Last week, young workers rioted in London to protest high taxes there. So that's how to get your message across!

The American dream?—The average price of a house in the city keeps going up and up. Lots of workers can't buy a home. So we have to rent to live here. The American dream used to be a job and a home. Now the dream is dreaming about a home and a job!!

This is some prize!—Last week, the big news was a company will build a plant in the nearby city to produce picture tubes and five other communities in three other states competed to get the plant. Now we're the winners but what did we win? Well, first we get to have the state pay the company $4.3 million to build here. Also, the city Council is creating a local Development Finance Authority just for the purpose of paying the company 3.3 million more. They say that the money will be taken from the taxes collected on the plant, which is another way of saying that it won't be going toward our water, sewer or other services. Guess who's going to pay? It won't be the company.

They're also getting a 50 % tax abatement for 12 years. What kind of prize is it when you have to pay for it?

The growing trend—More and more of us are doing the same thing. We grow up in this city, we go to school in the city. We get a job in the city, but we have to move out of the city because we can't afford to live here in the city.

Fair is fair—Workers in the machining department are being made to run 50% more machines. Management needs more workers trained in the classification so qualified setup men are forced to run 50% more machines and train a new worker at the same time. That's double the work. And what do we get out of it? If we are going to get double the work, we should get double the pay!

Break room Stupervisors—Remember the last newsletter article. " When does management work"? Well, now they put PCs in the breakrooms so stupervisors can sit in there all day and puff on cigarettes and drink coffee. What better way to get them out of our way! Of course we hope the odor from the bathrooms doesn't intoxicate them.

No profit—for workers—It's been half a year since our last bonus checks, even though most of us has been on time regularly. Every time the company makes a profit. They wind up buying new machines and poof, the profit disappears on the books anyway. If they can make a profit disappear that easy, why can't we do the same with the management?

"Someday, son, all of this can be yours!"

Computers vs. management—The company recently bought a stock inventory computer for big-bucks. The only problem is, it doesn't work. When it's up and running it works fine, but it's always breaking down. It's not working more than its working. But at least it's still pulling a better average than management!

When the lights go out—A storm knocked out the power at the plant for about 15 minutes, in April. All you could hear was whooping and hollering. No doubt about it, we enjoyed our extra break. We don't know but workers at the plant are pulling for more power outages. We can't wait for the next storm!

A poem—Roses are red, violets are blue. We pay the IRS, how about you?
Violets are blue, roses are red. Our faces are blue, and were in the red!

No chairs in Japan?—We workers at the plant have been doing a lot more standing while working in recent years, because we have been told "it is the way we do it in Japan". We know that's BS. They just want more work out of us. Management is quick to tell us about sitting. But why didn't they tell the new salesman walking around with us recently?! They were asking where are all the chairs, our feet are tired! Poor boys. That's what we go through all of our working lives.

When does management work?—Ever since top management at the plant made the policy of no smoking in the plant except in the cafeteria and the break rooms stupervisors are making their rounds from break room to break room to smoke. While workers are harassed over break times, etc. we're expected to jump at the sound of a bell!

Slim Perkin's—Salaried employees at the plant have met with union officials. Are they seeking representation? Maybe they are realizing all their perks aren't all they're cracked up to be!. The Union is looking better all the time!

Sick of it!—Five workers in the H-5 department went home sick last week. They were sick of an American foreman and a Japanese engineer working on the machines in their department. What makes them think they can run the machines right under three committeemen noses? Those jobs are for hourly workers. Next time, it could be an epidemic!

Weekend warriors or slaves?—While co-workers at the plant are feeling the effects of the recession. The corporation seems to be doing quite well. Word is they have purchased the building adjacent to the corporate office, where did they get the money?? From the profit sharing that were not going to get? Or the money they are saving on overtime by having all noncompliant parts sorted at the Tech Center instead of the plant? Maybe all those salaried people want a larger place to spend their weekends while sorting rejected parts.

It's spelled solidarity—It has been reported at the plant that some salary workers have been talking about joining a union. The reason given for organizing is mistreatment by some real ass in top management. We certainly wish them all the luck in the world in reaching for workplace dignity. We think it's a good solution. It's hard to change an ass, but we can change the system they work in.

The big Brown ones?—Two workers from the assembly area were suspended for five days. The foreman's walked through the area and only smelled Merryjoewana. One said that was enough proof of guilt, so home they went. But the office area smells like shit lately. Wonder what management has been smoking?

Let's soak their heads—At the plant, pollution is not a dirty word. It's been polluting the city for years. If it was up to us, the workers, we wouldn't have started polluting in the first place. We know what it means to our city and our families. Pollution is a dirty word, and the executives that run the company are even dirtier.

Who are they kidding?—When workers at the plant filed a grievance over profit sharing, the company denied it. They said they had no profit. Then how do they explain how they are getting new machinery? How are they building a new plant in another state? What do they do, buy all that with their losses?

He's dumber than we thought—Over 300 people were given service awards recently. But one general foreman was the only person to get booed. Instead of applauded. You'd think he'd get the message. But no, he thought it was a joke! Well, he passes the management stupidity test!

A parade, but no jobs—Many workers had family, friends and neighbors in the US military. They are glad the war is over and hoped their loved ones will be

Charlie Reed

home soon. Many of these people joined the military because they couldn't find a job. When they come home, they will find even fewer jobs than when they left. When the Vietnam vets came home. They got fewer jobs and no help from the government, which had sent them to war. The president talked a lot about supporting the troops, but he never supported these young people before he sent them to war. What will he do when they return?

Hazardous—A female security guard at the plant, who had been seeing a supervisor was fired. Don't be seen with management. It could be hazardous to your job!

The People's Hospital?—The company that owns our hospital in the city is planning to close it. But the workers are fighting the idea. There's been a rally and they're trying to get the community involved. People like the hospital. It's a good hospital that serves the community but the company thinks its profits are more important. Aren't hospitals supposed to be working for the community and not the other way around?

Make them pay this time!—Remember those promises, we heard last fall of complete job security in the new auto contracts? What a cruel joke. On top of that, there are hints that the auto companies want to reopen the contracts. We should be the ones who are fighting to reopen the contracts, we are the ones who will suffer hardship as unemployment continues. This time, let it be the executives and the big stockholders to make the concessions. To them it's only one more yacht or mansion. More or less. But to us, it's our daily bread.

<u>Whose vacation is it?</u>—The company is complaining about having less orders, so they're asking workers to take their vacation time now. Maybe that would be nice if you like skiing, but most of us plan our vacations for summer. And lately there isn't even enough snow to ski on!

<u>A riddle</u>—What do x-plants, x—cars and x-executives brains have in common? Answer: they're working one week, off the next, working one week, off the next. Then again, maybe were giving the executives too much credit!

<u>G.I. Joe</u>—The company hired a military man who earn the Nick name G.I. Joe. He runs the department as if it were a military operation. Everybody is expected to attend all morning meetings. It's gotten so bad that one of the workers wears fatigues! Most workers are showing signs of AWOL tendencies. Let's toss him a SCUD!

<u>Company logic</u>—At the plant, all of the overtime comes in the summer. When we could be enjoying ourselves outside instead of in the winter. When we'd want to be inside anyway, if we would just work through the winters we could have all sorts of time off in the summer and the company wouldn't have to complain about absenteeism, but they're not that logical.

<u>Try paying something decent</u>—The city used to hire a security agency that paid its workers $3.75 an hour to patrol the city parking lots, but they weren't happy with the service they got. Now, they hire their own security guards, and they pay a little more, but it's still not a

living wage. Just like this city. They expect security, but they won't give it to the workers.

Make it big—Management recently fired a worker for putting out $1000 worth of scrap. Meanwhile management just lost $1.7 million worth of parts . . . . poof, up in smoke. And nobody's head rolled for that! The lesson, make sure your mistake is really big. Then you'll be safe!

Big scary's dream—At the plant, a new plant slogan was proposed at a recent plant wide meeting. It was "work harder to make Big Scary look smarter", but we can't work that hard. Nobody can work that hard!

Fund for the greedy—The company held its annual raffle to raise money for its fund for the needy. And this year, workers gave a record amount. So what did the company do? It held back more than it gave out! What will the company do with all that money, make interest all year long? Management turned our fund for the needy, into a fund for the greedy!

20 mistakes a month—The company has reported an average of 20 mistakes a month, all in taking customer orders and relating them to manufacturing. Boy, those folks must be Big Scary's relatives because if we made those many mistakes in manufacturing. We'd be out the door!

This is quality?—Quality month was celebrated at the plant by handing out buttons. The buttons said "the company and the union quality for today and tomorrow and beyond". But tomorrow was misspelled on the buttons! That's par for the course. The company can't even talk about quality without screwing something up.

A well-deserved meal—On December 11, the company gave free holiday dinners for the retirees. Since they couldn't find it in their hearts to give the retirees COLA and with some retirees getting a pension of less than $100 a month. A few more free meals wouldn't hurt. A lot of workers here like visiting with the retirees. Maybe the company should give them a meal every day!

Cost-saving measures—The plant manager just recently went to the supers and told them to come up with three cost-saving measures for each department. Gee, we can think of one big cost-saving measure, right there.

Sheriff Dog—We've got our own Dep. Dog at the plant. The poor feller just lopes around all of the time trying to catch that muskrat. And he's always leaving his bones and doggy damage all over the place. But now he's in the fix.. What's he going to do with all those chairs he rustled up? How is he going to fit all those chairs in his doghouse?

We don't have to take it—Workers at the plant, kept the thieves at bay with our latest contract. The company was trying to force co-pays on pensions and HMOs. But the workers voted down the contract proposal twice. The company gave a little. Now there is no co-pays on HMOs. It's not a great contract, but it's a lot better than we would have gotten if we'd caved in sooner. And the bargaining committee told us it wouldn't do any good to insist on more!

Charlie Reed

Who's complaining?—Foreman are complaining about their salaries. They're bent out of shape because after overtime the production workers supposedly make more than they do. And you know, they'd like to think they're more important to the company than we are. Aw . . . too bad, do they think they work harder than we do? Were doing all the work while they just stand around and shoot off their mouths. What more do they want?

Pigs in a trough—When the company moved their plant from the city to the township. They got their 50% tax abatement over 12 years. Then got their concessions from the Union. Now there making profits like crazy, and they still keep coming after the workers for more. Well, this plant was built on a cornfield, so when are we going to get the pigs out of the trough?

Work smarter not harder—We got a new company president last year. The funny thing is he's always telling us to work smarter not harder, but we work harder and he works smarter. Maybe we ought to follow his advice and stop killing ourselves. And if a foreman asks us what the deal is, we'll just tell him, we're working smarter not harder!

Break time—A lot of workers are developing hand problems from the constant, hard work. Also, the fumes from the machines make it hard to breathe. Its funny how the front offices are always well ventilated. Come to think of it. It's well ventilated outside the plant too. If we just can't breathe in the plant. We just might be forced to take air break!

A poem—At the company they operate a heartless way, they try and make the workers pay. They run around like they know what they're doing, but we know and us, they're not fooling. We can work harder like we're part of a team and squeal on co-workers like were part of the scheme. But the bosses are getting richer and thicker and were not working smarter, but only harder. So support workers rights, and don't get uptight. If we stayed together, we can't lose this fight!

New slogan—Our version of the plant slogan: Company/Union-Sorting today, Tomorrow, and beyond!

Plant manager: A Turkey or a ham?—It would be nice if the company would give us a turkey or a ham for Thanksgiving. They probably could afford both and we deserved both. But we really don't expect the plant manager's chest to fly open and his heart to fall out!

Plant safety—don't choke on it!—In the grind and machining areas in the plant we always had a problem with oil mist and smoke. Back in 1988 management told us that mist collectors would be installed to take care of the mist. It will be 1992 soon, and that's four years since they agreed to do it. Remember that when your foreman asks you to do something for them.

The wrong solution—At the plant a Charity had a hot dog lunch day to help raise funds for the charity campaign, can't they pick a better menu instead of asking us to choke down hotdogs. We should not need to help people through charitable contributions anyway, we should be providing jobs that pay a living wage. The charity is actually the bosses way.

How big is her head?—One foreman thinks she knows more than the other foreman in the plant. And she even tells the other shifts, what to do. She's got a big head. If you don't believe it just ask her. We need a good nickname for her, any suggestions?

Bulletin board—There was a problem before the election. The union said the bulletin board could only be used to represent one point of view. Well, there was a meeting, and now we have . . . . a bulletin board with a lock and key. We used to think some action was better than no action.

Top-secret—There's a rumor that the company wants to change the scheduling around and go to a four-day week with less over time. But the company isn't saying anything. We thought the MOA meant we could make decisions about our work. But how can we make decisions if the company treats everything as top secret? Anyway, if the company tells us what they want to do, then the workers still have to agree to it, right? Last year, even without the MOA, a group of workers who didn't want this plan said no and the company couldn't do it. It should be that much easier to say no now, if the MOA is what they say it is.

Weekends—Management has a lot of nerve. They tell us to come in and work on the weekends and they are never even here on the weekends. That isn't right. But what else can we expect. Their motto is, "do as I say, not as I do".

Labor Day—It was nice to have a couple of days off. It gives us a chance to get reacquainted with our families and do the things we like to do. But Labor Day only comes once a year and we deserve Labor Day's more often than that.

Greed at our expense—Six new jobs were posted for the assembly department. We heard there are a few grind set up workers that are signing into assembly. They're going to force grinders to run three machines soon, an increase of one third of the work load. But they're increasing our work loads all over the plant. Cutting out stupervisors jobs because of the MOA. Look at all the money they'll be saving and making, but who will get all the money? We will be getting the extra work and they'll getting the Money!

Seems like we missed something?—Our bargaining committee wanted to know in the membership contracts survey back in May of this year. If we were willing to do a list of things. They were : #1 attend all meetings #2 willing to strike if necessary #3 hand out leaflets #4 file grievances #5 wear T-shirts on T-shirt day #6 wear union buttons #7 sign petitions. Well, were still ready!

Heavyweight moved to scrap—The plant manager found Eachy a new job as head scrap man in the plant. The people he's over have our deepest sympathy! We're sure scrap will take on a new meaning and will become more important than ever.

Slow getting started—The MOA must be coming soon. So maybe the stupervisors will be so busy backstabbing other stupervisors, they will stay off our ass.

Charlie Reed

Hired as "bathroom watcher" will travel—We don't know if you know it or not, but there is a bathroom watcher on second shift. He sits around claiming you're the one who's wasting company time. But anyone that watches bathrooms like bathroom watcher we know who's wasting company time! Maybe it's his weird way of trying to convince the company heads that he's needed!

Crumbs for living—COLA increase for September will be four cents. Wow! We don't think 4 cents will pay for the increased cost of coffee or gas or food or for that matter the increase in electricity. Not to mention cigarettes.

Generally speaking—Seems that Sticky Fingers wants to make sure in her memo that she's is a general stupervisor. The only general thing about her is she generally can't make the right decision, generally makes an ass out of herself, and generally doesn't know what's going on.

Better stand back—Why is it they tell us we are going to do away with stupervisors. Then hire two at the same time? It looks like another time, the company is blowing it out there ass, again.

Healthy habits?—Does the front office pay Crablegs salary based on how many cigarettes he can chain smoke in the cafeteria all day long?

One ringy dingy—When the inspectors asked for a phone in their old and now new office. Absolutely was the answer. Butterfly, sticky fingers, and G.I. Joe all had different answers. Seems a new phone showed up in the label maker office but none for the inspectors. When asked why and how the inspectors got the runaround, see nothing, hear nothing, know nothing. This has a familiar ring to it

<u>Trip hazard</u>—The front step is a safety hazard. Everyone making deliveries to that door has problems. Why not make it easier on everyone and cement a long incline. Say to the front gate that would cost less than an accident!

<u>And they talk about crime!</u>—The electrical panels are left open on MA's in assembly because they heat up then don't operate properly or stop. So back panels are left open to help cool them down. Why? It's against OSHA regulations. But when has the company ever really worried about following the law!

<u>Ratification meetings should be open</u>—There were some fellow workers at the ratification meeting that didn't want to hear all the questions that were asked. Apparently their minds were made up. But why do they get so mad and say those workers are crying. Maybe they want a speechless meeting, where no one can ask questions, where we just vote.

<u>Big dummies!</u>—There were some good and funny jokes posted up around the plant recently. It's good to see we still have a sense of humor after looking at our agreement. Why do we have to work harder to get a weekend off? And how hard is the front office working to get every weekend off? How long will it take for them to figure it out? We are not working harder, only smarter!

<u>We need to put up a fight</u>!—S&A or sick leave pay was increased from $200 a week to $275 a week, but it has cost us 26 weeks to get that increase because the weeks were to be reduced to 26 weeks. So now let's see, if you're sick and can't work maybe home laying in bed. We will only get about half a paycheck for six months. For most of us, we live from paycheck to paycheck. So what are we going to do without money after that? Maybe we can look to our "friend" in Washington for help. I know it was a bad joke, isn't it.

<u>Right to know laws</u>—Did you know, the company must provide workers with a written hazard communication program that defines responsibilities, contains a complete list of hazardous chemicals present in the workplace, inform workers of the hazards of a non-routine tasks and demonstrates how to identify the contents of in-house pipes and piping systems? Looks like the company has a little work to do. Or maybe they don't care about the safety laws.

<u>Mushrooms</u>—What's going on with our contract? They have been already negotiating for three weeks, we still haven't heard anything? Like it's not our contract. They are treating us like mushrooms . . . they keep us in the dark and only feed us bull.

<u>Remember when?</u>—Quality through involvement and problem solving or Q-tips. This was our quality circles program back in the olden days. Good riddance! Big Scary told us the mist collectors in grind would take out 95% of the mist out of the air. What a big lie!

<u>M. D.???</u>—Management should open a clinic, and let Band-Aid queen operate it and do all the diagnoses. She knows more than our doctors. If she gets a diagnosis wrong, she can just hand the patient a shovel!

<u>He makes a mother proud</u>—Looks like top management is aiming to get the fat out of lower management. They're passing out jobs surveys and asking them to list all of their duties. That's funny, Eachy's will be a blank piece of paper. We don't believe he would write what he really does, harassing workers, writing up people and finding someone to push around.

<u>Alcoholics anonymous</u>—Well, we had inventory. It would have went well alright if Eachy hadn't come in smelling like a brewery and aggravating people. He must have been out partying with his stoned-head buddies

<u>Worker wins!</u>—Sticky fingers took a worker's newsletters he had been collecting up for some time. And guess what, personnel made her give them back! Mark one up for us and free speech!

<u>Special delivery</u>—Hey Sticky Fingers, we hear you had a little trouble lifting the last copy of the newsletter. Now you know . . . all you had to do is ask for it, and you'll get it. You won't have to steal it from the workers here anymore.

<u>Salary perks</u>—There must be something wrong with the Plant manager's legs. The poor man has to park his car by the front entrance every day. How did he win his reserved parking place?

The company's "Golden rule"—Did you know that while you were eating. a cold sandwich and chips. Your salaried leaders were hiding in the dark scarfing their pizza down in fear that you might want a piece? Didn't their mothers teach them to share with others?

All out scrap hunt!—Call the guards! Send in the troops! Keep no prisoners! Showed no mercy! And weld a cap over the scrap hopper and keep it locked! Now, the stage is set. All eyes will be on him, the one sorry worker that tries to scrap a part without making out a scrap ticket. An unthinkable crime against all of management and corporate profits. The nerve, you must have!

Wishy-washer—What happen to health and safety in the assembly department? Online 25. The washer is making workers sick, headaches, dizziness and itchy skin are just a few of the problems. You can call the company environmentally friendly, but to us. That's a joke!

We heard—Management is dreaming up a new salary absentee policy. We're sure it will be a loosely monitored policy. And we hear they are also dreaming up one for us too. We want the same policy as Stupervisor Romeo on second shift has. Need we say more?

Problems? We don't see problems!—When we asked questions about quality because we think we found some bad parts. Why does management act like we have a problem and not the parts? Oh well . . . we don't have to ask any more questions do we?

Springtime is never fun—This spring and early summer seems like a good time to take that long awaited time off. Now, before they put in place the new absentee policy. So, pick a nice day and have fun!!!

MOA? Not okay!—A modern operating agreement for the company? Why? They can't even live up to the old agreement! Do stupervisors really have any power? So why would you think the company would bestow real power on us? They've already given us the stockman's job. The janitor's job. The inspectors job, the operator's job and parts of the machine repair job and they've combined classifications. Now, something comes along called "empowerment", and they want to give us a stupervisors job also!

Greed is out of control!—They made the workers in the heat treat department run the new belt furnace without any extra help. Which doubled the furnace operators workload. 100% increase in workload is far too much to do. That kind of speed up should be against the law.

Who's the Asshole?—An engineer in the heat treat department has called a furnace operator a asshole because he was writing on his inspection sheet the word "missed". Which is what happens when they double their workload. Some things have to be missed. Why would the engineer gets so mad? He doesn't have to do the work!

Progress?—Since the company increased production, we will have even more overtime. Can we really call this way of life progress? So many of us are on seven days a week now. Hell, even slaves got Sunday off and even those Auto workers slaves get Sunday off. All this overtime is going to have its cost on our lives, more divorces, more accidents, which we already see and more pressure, pressure, pressure!!

"It looks good around here with all the flowers and stuff. But there's very little shade since they took down the barbed-wire!"

<u>Migrate to clean air</u>—Why does the company allows so much oil mist in the grind areas? It stinks and in the winter, everything is closed off. So, it's hard to breathe that crap into our lungs. Sure, the company can clean the mist collectors again and again, but they don't have to work in this mess. Look at the build up on the ceiling and pipes. We don't have clean air out by our machines, so we need to spend more time in the break rooms, where the air is cleaner.

<u>Always at the top</u>—Well, we had our yearly meeting with Big Scary. He looked good in his fancy new suit. He told us how well we did last year, then on the other hand, he told us how great a benefit package we have. I wonder how great his benefit packages is? Maybe big scary doesn't know the workers are not the company's enemy. I don't care how many fancy new suits Big Scary has or how much his bonuses are. He'll always be right at the top with the likes of Robber Barons.

<u>Needs real help</u>—Seems like Dim-Wit is really losing it. Is his job really getting to him? Looks like he needs some help and real soon, before he and Eachy start looking alike. Let's hope Stormin-Welder takes his blood pressure pills before he blows a gasket or trips over himself charging after the workers from shipping.

<u>No profits?</u>—Wow! Have you seen the new copy machine? It looks out of this world! They bought it at the end of the year. Must mean they need to hide profits, trying to have more tax write offs. A spaceship just landed in the front office! No, that's the new copy machine!

Charlie Reed

Blind ambition—The company raffle should join with the workers to help more of their own. Giving the money to the charities doesn't make sense, when there are workers on S&A, that could use the help.

Petition—A probationary worker was fired recently. A petition went around to get him rehired, that got over 100 signatures. It was sent to Big Scary. We'll see how fair he is. As we all know, actions speak louder than words.

Just working for a living—Why does management keep telling us to change over the lines? Setups take a lot of time and they are always crying about getting more parts out. They tell us changeover to this part number, then change back to the other part number. If you can't get the parts that's on one machine to run, don't take the time to get it running right, go on to the next part number. Of course, we get paid by the hour and we can thank the union for that. But it's a wonder. Why cry about numbers so much and do all this setup time, and money wasting. It looks like they'll never change, so maybe we should get them a big handkerchiefs for Christmas, so they can have a big cry.

Don't blame the company . . . not!!—We couldn't help notice that when the chemist gave the hazardous chemical class, she seemed to always blame chemicals we use in our homes or while pumping gas or changing oil. Of course, we know she knows there are hazardous chemicals in the plant too. So why did she try to avoid talking about them? There is a whole book full in the MSDS books around the plant that are filled with the chemicals we use right here in the plant.

A freak show—Ever watch Eachy when he's trying to communicate to someone? Stop and watch some time. It can be fun. He waves his hands all about, and points his fingers. If you watch closely, you can see his head turn red. We might think he's got something inside he wants to say to us. Oh well who knows? Someone may listen to him someday!!

We don't believe it—Why are we working weekends when the plant is over 100% production? We were told if we work hard and ran more production, we wouldn't have to work the weekends. Apparently that was a lie!

Abuse of power—Drugs at the plant, maybe. Could the police be investigating? Its possible. They have done it at other plants around the area, but all they turn up with and end up coming after is the users and the smalltime dealers. Police should spend our tax dollars in a more effective way. Like finding out why so many people in the plant are getting heart attacks or cancer. Why go after the smalltime dealer and the users? It's easier. Or do they want to leave the big timers alone so they can get paid off and then arrest some people using and selling small quantities.

It helps to get to know each other—There have been a lot of job postings lately, and a lot of us have been signing up for them. Changing jobs gives us a chance to meet new people and to learn new things. Of course, management is the same all over the plant. Like we do twice as many setups as we need to, or the tooling you need is not the right size, etc. etc. But of course we don't let that stand in our way when we want a new job!

<u>Christmas raffle</u>—The companies sickness and accident is so bad, and pays so little each week that workers feel compelled to have a raffle to help out during Christmas time.

<u>OSHA came, OSHA saw, OSHA fined!</u>—OSHA has fined the company thousands of dollars. Wow, it was more than a slap on the wrist. And we even had a class about the "right to know" Law's and MSDSs. But we should have the "right to decide" about workplace chemicals not just the right to know

<u>Take a real break</u>—Some people are fighting for a smoke-free break room. For a real break from work, we ought to fight for a stupervisor free break rooms too!

<u>Waaaaaa, I want to go to Chicago</u>—The company needed someone to go to Chicago to address a customer complaint last week. G.I. Joe really wanted to go, but the company sent someone with great intellect instead.

<u>Our loss</u>—A longtime worker in the front office has passed away recently. Back in the 80s, she was fired and then had to fight to get her job back. And when she was hired back, the company put her out in the guard house, as a guard. They told her it was the only job open. In March, she felt pressured to retire. The company wanted to reduce payroll dollars in the front office, but did they? Now management acts as if they mourn her death. Why? Stress and pressure is the number one killer, and that's all they gave to her!

<u>The fickle finger of fate</u>—Why does the company think it's sabotage when the customer gets bad parts? The only sabotage is when management chooses profit over quality. If they want to point fingers, let them point fingers at themselves. We are certainly giving them the finger.

<u>Chair wars</u>—Seems like Eachy is back to the war of the chairs. God for bid, if some of our fellow employees would feel a little better if they want to take their feet off the cement floors for just a few minutes. Eachyism is not just a word at the company. Why would this company keep and pay the likes of him? Certainly there must be someone at the company's upper management that can see the tremendous loss of production because of the poor attitudes caused by Eachyism. There goes our profit sharing!

<u>Saving money . . . on private eyes</u>—The company had us make out forms, so they can update their computer records on us, why? They probably know more about us than we do! They just want to know how correct, it is. Could it be they're trying to help us out . . . not!

<u>A solution, but?</u>—With all due respect to workers that smoke, why does management demand that people only smoke in the break rooms and the cafeteria. If the company really wants to keep a safe work environment. Why not have smoking only in the production areas? That way keeping a smoke-free environment in the break rooms and cafeteria. But that might satisfy both groups and the company couldn't stand for that!

<u>They're only doing their stupid jobs</u>—Why is the company nitpicking people. They seem to pick people out and start harassing them for nothing. To them, it

doesn't matter if you play golf with them or sit on a voluntary Christmas committee with them. You could go to parties with them and go out drinking with management. But when it comes to in plant discipline, even if you they know what you're doing is wrong they'll still come after you. All that matters to them is the corporation!.

Show and tell—Eachy showed pictures of rags all over P2, why didn't someone show him pictures of him showing off his — in the Department years ago?

Serious about scrap?—Now, we are hearing a lot of from management about all the scrap dollars loss. But the dollar amounts are meaningless because there are areas where they don't monitor it. How concerned can they be about the problem when they leave the scrap man's job empty when he is on vacation or sick leave?

Let the good Times roll—Now that the Cold War is over, we no longer live under the threat of Soviet communism. But the workers at the plant live under a more painful threat, Eachyism. It is meant to agitate, disrupt and deflate one's self-esteem. When is the real management going to remove this roadblock? Hourly and salaried employees alike ask, why is he still here? Quite a mystery. The consensus says fire him. Then maybe the plant can finally have a good year.

The lies are funny!—Before, we have been told, we weren't making a profit because they couldn't sell enough bearings. Now were told, it's because we don't hit 100% production every month. And what will be their next excuse, we don't hit a hundred pieces per man-hour?

How nice they are, not!—We got a weekend off. Were they being nice? Let's pretend they were!

Protect your health!—If you're overworked or your
boss is a jerk.
Restriction . . . restriction . . . restriction
If you're working 12 hours a day and have forgotten how to cook.
Restriction . . . restriction . . . restriction
If your family asks your name and you show your photo ID.
Restriction . . . restriction . . . restriction
If you're ready to blow off steam and all you have is bad luck.
Restriction . . . restriction . . . restriction
If you're full of pain pills and need a rest.
Restriction . . . restriction . . . restriction

Cram management—Why did the company cram so many machines into such a small area as P6 grind? Why didn't management ask us what we thought? What happened to employee involvement? What happened to action teams? We need to work together all right. But without management!

Second class citizens—III Pill posted a letter that workers are to stop moving their cars up out in the parking lot on company time. But how many personal things does management do on company time? And we don't see III Pill taking an hour to type up that letter!

The animal king-dumb—Why did they fire two probationary workers the Friday before last? What did they do, that was so wrong? Did they give the employees any warnings or did they pounce on them like an animal looking for its prey? What's the big secret about, who was behind their firings? But we know, we know.

If we fight each other, the company has an easy—There is so much fighting among each other in the plant, the company doesn't even have to come against us. We can't seem to get it together and stop fighting each other. The company must love it, all the while playing one worker against the other. If we don't stop, our union will be lost.

Post-personnel jobs now!—The only jobs we've seen posted on the board are salaried jobs. Why aren't they posting hourly jobs anymore? It looks like they're trying to hire workers into utility jobs, and then just place them into non-interchangeable jobs without posting them. Of course personnel knows better than that, right . . . wrong.

A postal problem?—When Eachy is going around trying to piss you off, what right does he have to do that and where does it come from? Has he worked for the US Postal Service before? If someone goes off on him, we won't be surprised.

OSHA?—Whatever happened to the OSHA results? The guy takes two or three weeks to go through the plant and is never heard of again. Maybe he got a toxic dose of the company. Maybe the company doesn't give a shit about his findings.

Quick . . . call a meeting!—Quality management seems to think all problems can be solved by having a meeting when a customer is unhappy because they got some bad parts. And so what does management do?

A bunch of chicken little—Grievances are backlogged to say the least. The company always needs a lot of time to follow our contract. Only a few get solved quickly. Sit on them, sit on them. What's the company trying to do, hatch them?

They get what they pay for—Big Scary came in to complain to plant management about how production has dropped recently. Hmmm . . . workers get harassed, and production goes down. Could there be a connection there? Nahh!

Hall monitors—Did anyone see the safety tour going around lately? How could we miss them, they told us all individually as they went around. Gee, that gives me a warm feeling all over, I must be coming down with something!

Tensions building—A worker on first shift was suspended because she supposedly threatened an inspector. Even if this is true, the company is responsible. Management has been provoking all of us, by increasing quotas and putting people under a lot of stress and pressure. Under these conditions, it was only a matter of time, sooner or later someone was bound to explode. There's probably a lot more of us ready to do the same thing. Next time let's all explode together, against the real problem.

Flea bitten—We didn't hear the dog barking a couple weeks ago. He was on vacation in his doghouse.

But what happened to the Tie?—The uniforms the company has on display in the cafeteria doesn't need to be under lock and key because nobody would want to steal them anyway!

We don't need them, they need us—The new machines in P5 don't run like they should. We have a solution. Let the operators run the machines and get the stupervisors and the engineers out of the department. But we know, the company won't listen and we don't mind standing around watching them.

Since when does the company Panhandle?—We all just got a cola increase of eight cents an hour. But we only saw four cents of it because the company took four cents for a little bit more of a retirement plan. That four cents an hour adds up with all the built in increases that will be over $21,000 in 10 years, for each one of us. For those of us who will be around that long, will be paying the company over $71,000 in the next 30 years for our own retirement package. Is that package worth that kind of money? Look around, you don't see people rushing to retire do you?

Live and learn—The tour Queens didn't do so well with the company tour. He didn't immediately fall in love with them or the plant. He wanted to actually see our quality systems!

A better way—Were in a vicious circle. All this overtime affects our family life. So we try to adjust by taking time off to spend time with their families. Then we get angry and get disciplined, because we took more time off and it puts more pressure on us to work more and work faster. And we take more time off, just to try to live and on and on. We could reduce our burden by giving work to all the unemployed. And all those who are the bosses would be expected to put in their fair share. There is a better way and we workers can make it.

An injury to all—The company is trying to divide us, and weaken us. The workers on third shift are under attack. Right now, the rest of us may think there is nothing to worry about. It's only the third shift. It's only workers with absentee problems. But we could be next. If they get away with it with some of us, it's easier for them to come after the rest of us. Pretty soon they'll be putting the screws on all of us. The company tries to tell some of us that there is nothing we can do to defend ourselves but wait for the grievance procedure. And they tell the rest of us, it's not our worry. But we all have an interest in fighting an attack and we all have ways to fight it now.

It's a slugfest—Why was only half of the plant told to get coffee and donuts? Didn't they buy enough for all of us? We may have seen our last donut. The war has started, harassment is up, production is down, where will it end?

Our environment—The company just spent a lot of money on a new trash compactor, but there is a lot more trash that could be recycled than is currently. They could have saved the money and help our environment at the same time.

Overtime condos—It would sure help our family life, if the company built condos for us in the field nearby. But don't look for it.

Backwards Bob—Bob-down doesn't want to look bad, and so he is competing with the other shifts, so he is writing up people and sending people home. But what he doesn't realize is, we don't come to work or stay home to make him look good. He is competing with other stupervisors, just like they want us to do, trying to run more production than the other shifts. If he wanted more production, he should have been more operative with us. Instead, production is down. People are angry and Bob-down is afraid to walk out in the plant.

Navy flier—The company has their own navy flyer, he is GI-low. Now we can understand why he thinks so little of the women under his wing and above his wing. Maybe the US congressional committee should be notified of his whereabouts. He should be reported immediately!

A rhyme—OT . . . OT go away, give it to us in straight time pay, and we need more time for weekend play!

Newsletter SOP—Process of Reporting, if you are:
> Harassed by a stupervisors
> Forced to run many machines
> Nitpicked over lunches and break times
> Discriminated against
> Sick of their innuendoes
> Overworked and underpaid

Spread the word to your coworkers :
> Tell the newsletter person
> Write up an article
> Submit a cartoon
> Send in a letter

The pressure makes us sick—Recently the dog has told us the pressure is on about running production, as if all the OT wasn't pressure enough. Now the company is starting to worry and wonder about all of the absenteeism. Is the company stupid or what? Good thing, we aren't!

The name says it all—Mr. Lame-O knows and must agree with the way Eachy treats workers in the plant. He has been told many times by many different workers how Eachy treats us and the way he pushes us to run bad quality. It should show us that we can't rely on Mr. Lame-O to wake up and see the light.

Why can't they be fair?—Discrimination has shown its ugly head before at the company. Now it's showing its beastly head again. Who set the rules, or do they make them up as they go.

Assholes don't make good friends—Stupervises on third shift are threatening to move some of us because we work well together and talk. We don't mind, unlike them, we make friends easily.

Don't leave the door open—The Quality dragon is chasing management out of the building, or did someone let in Eachy.

We're not animals—Some people on second and third shifts are getting angry at all the overtime and they're putting in for 40 hour restrictions. So now the supervisors have started nitpicking us on every minute of lunch and breaks. Since they can't work us like mules, they're treating us like dogs. Well, they ain't seen the jackass in us yet!

That's incredible—The plant wide meeting should be in the Guinness world book of records. According to the Plant manager. This plant showed no profits over the 50 years it's been here. And yet, here it is, still in operation. Or maybe he meant to say we workers haven't made any money in the last 50 years. Maybe they lived on tax abatements from the city and concessions from the workers.

Hit the door, Pill—Out-the-door Pill is going around asking when some of us workers are going to retire. The question should be . . . when is he going to retire?

No excuses—Eachy was called home early one Friday because of a leaky hot water heater. Where's his plumbers excuse?

Vending machine blues—A worker was fired for going out to lunch instead of eating out of the machines here. Figures. He was fired for showing some intelligence.

He got a bang out of it—.You might not want to offer the Dog a cigarette . . . he's probably a little gun shy!!

We didn't miss him—We didn't have any arguments, and the plant ran fairly smooth. Which manager was off last week? Was Eachy on vacation?

Can't he find something constructive to do?—Eachy sat at his desk all day and worked out production requirements for each production line on a daily basis, as if we are to make their production goals. HA HA HA HA HA HA HA !!!

Down to Earth, is more than clothes—Everybody in the corporate office wears casual clothes every Friday. Jeans and T-shirts. They want to show how "down to Earth" they are. Gee, how nice of them. And maybe we should have a dress-up day and wear suits and dresses on the lines each Friday to show support for there "head in the clouds" management. Well, maybe not!

Brilliant move—Peter Cottontail flooded the heat treat dept. with water during shutdown. They had to pump it all out, at a cost of 20 cents a gallon. It froze up eight motors. Did he get written up? Oh that's right, he's a stupervisor.

Ask the experts—The only good engineers, we have around here are the older ones. We set up people don't have time to train the younger ones!

In their dreams—Well, now the steak dinner is scheduled for August 3. Yeah, that's a lot better than getting those profit-sharing checks we used to get! Not!

Charlie Reed

Take out the clowns—When someone is hired on the shop floor, they may be yet a quick mention on the bulletin boards. But when a salaried person is hired. They get a picture, and a big write up on their histories, their education and their likes and dislikes etc.. Who cares? We'd rather hear about our coworkers, not those bozos.

We agree with Big Scary—In Big Scary spare time he's been doing some reading about peak performance. We agree we need peak performance. We need peak performance on grievances. We need peak performance on safety, when we tell the stupervisor. And yes, we need peak performance in our paychecks!!

Mission : impossible—Why is Eachy trying to buddy up with certain people, talking and laughing with them? Is he trying to make friends? Well, he's wasting his breath. If he wants to make friends, he'll have to stop acting like Mr. Company.

We can't do everything—If management wants more production, why don't they hire more janitors to help keep our floors mopped up? They've already got us running all the machines, keeping size ,checking quality, making out paperwork and on and on and on. So they think were magicians, or what? With all the jobs to do, we have to be extra careful not to make any mistakes, and if it takes more time, oh well.

Good for something—Thanks Eachy, you really helped us get union support. The new hires were asking for union T-shirts before they even got their 90 days in!

Mental pause—We weren't back before a sign appeared saying the plant is 50% behind production, because we took two weeks off? Now they're saying we have to work on weekends to catch up. Yeah, sure. How many years have we been shutting down in July, and they still can't plan ahead for this. Gee, they should find the person in charge of this and get rid of them, if they are really that stupid.

Get back to us when you decide—We're so confused! One shift stupervisor want us to do one thing, and then another shift stupervisor tell us something else. And were caught in the middle wondering what to do. We should be able to do what we know is best, not do whatever, just to stroke the stupervisor's ego. We'll just have to step back and wait for them to work it out between themselves.

They can't walk and chew gum—Did you know the one out of every five workers at our plant is a salary worker? Of course we need some but we have twice as many stupervisors and three times as many engineers as we need. How many stupervisors and engineers does it take to screw in a lightbulb? Far too many!!

A real stuper-visor—We couldn't help but notice that one of the newly promoted stupervisors has a tattoo: "cocaine" it says. Leave it to management to send out mixed signals. So it's wrong for us, but okay for them? Are they going to put him in charge of drug testing now?

Jim Beam's worried about our safety glasses. We're worried about his prescription!

<u>United we stand</u>—Why does the company require a diagnosis on our doctors notes? What about our privacy. We have laws that protect us against doctors giving out information. Doesn't the company respect the law and us? But why would we hope for that, they don't even abide by our union contract!

<u>Move along and let us work</u>—Every time Eachy comes into the shop floor, production drops like clockwork. People say, as long as he's around my machines, I'm not running them. If the company wants to keep production up, they ought to keep Eachy where he's most useful, held away in his office.

<u>No joke</u>—Management said the North end of the plant would be getting air conditioning, they lie. Now we will be getting only "conditioned" air, just air blown in from the outside. Then management had the nerve to laugh about it, when we ask about it. They must think that our working conditions are a joke. We aren't laughing.

<u>The blind leading the dumb</u>—G.I. Joe has gone to second shift to help train stupervisors on that shift. Good luck! They are all gonna and need it!

<u>Misinformation</u>—Did you see the notice the company posted on the bulletin board about drug testing? According to them, most of the workers are for it now, because the tests are more accurate, and because workers resent drug use by fellow workers. Where do they get this stuff? Sure we don't like drug use on the lines, because it might affect our safety. And we know there are better ways to deal with job stress. But we're not about to blame our coworkers. If we resent

anything, it's the pressure were all under, to work harder and faster, pressure that drives some of us to do drugs. We blame the company. And just because we don't like drug use on the line. That doesn't mean we like giving up our privacy to the company. Keep your noses in your own damn urine!

I'll be good mommy—Hey Eachy, there is some chairs in the locker rooms. Hope it makes you mad. Why can't you leave our chairs alone? Do you have hangups over chairs? Did your mother puts you in a chair when you were bad. And now you don't want anyone in a chair? Thanks, but no thanks. Now go sit in the corner!

He's trying to cover his trail—Why does Peter Cottontail wear blue overalls? Is he trying to fool us into thinking he's working? But then again, we can expect that out of a old used car salesman!

They're good for nothing—Some stupervisors don't know the difference between an assembly, grind or machine blueprint and some have worked on the shop floor for many years. It shows how little is thought of quality in management. How can we put out a good bearing out the door when stupervisors don't even know the basics? But we don't need them to make bearings, do we!

They should come out more often!—It would be nice if the company put umbrellas up over the picnic tables. What kind of shut-in thought to plant that kind of tree with very little leaves. A nice maple tree the same height would make a good shade tree, but why would they do that, it makes too much sense. Those trees out front give as much shade as the chain-link fence and the barbed wire over it!

They know where to find us—Now that the mist collectors and air-conditioning are running, management is saying, no eating, drinking or smoking in the plant. Gee, that must mean more trips to the break rooms!

Cow chip committee—Now that management has taken our chairs out of the work areas, production is down. Gee, it is hard to figure out that if they make us stand up all day. Our work will suffer. But Eachy won't learn until he sets up another one of those cow chip committees to study the problem.

Creamed banana—Banana Mike has been telling us the plant may have to keep running Memorial Day weekend, to catch up on production. You know, banana mike, the long, squishy guy with all the fruit flies around his head. Well, if he wants to work Memorial Day weekend so bad, we hope he has fun. And if he can run the whole plant by himself, then more power to him!

Another bright idea—Can you believe it, management is giving us absorbent pads to the put under the carts to soak up the oil, instead of fixing the carts from leaking. And where will they want us to put those used pads, in the trash, to do more polluting? We ought to be putting them on the bosses chairs.

Equality . . . we deserve it—Eachy says he wants to treat everyone as equals. Lets see, Eachy spends all his time in the break room's, smoking. Hey, can we be as equal as Eachy is?

Eachy is a Z defect—Quality problems are normal in a plant like ours, running close tolerances. But there are many more problems lately since Eachy came on board. We don't blame him for all the Rust, scale, bad seals, nicks, bad ODs, narrower races, flakes on faces, race and OD not cleaned up. We'll blame him for most that gets to the customer and sent back. If you have to ask why, you haven't talked to him about quality.

Bring out the clowns—No wonder the company can't get enough workers to help out during open-house. Why should we, would you want to work with Eachy and the brotherhood? So management will have to man most of the jobs. And the kids will love to see all our clowns!

Justice for all?—Management is buying all new chairs for the front offices and throwing out ours. Looks like another example of Eachy equality.

Making decisions—Workers in the north end of the plant are being made to enter their daily productions into the PCs. But that was the stupervisor's job before. We are doing more work, so why aren't we given $.50 more an hour? It's because management is only going to pay just so much, no matter how much work we do or how much profit we make for them. So, if management wants big numbers, we know how to give it to them, right?

Our-way is better—Since we heard all about the scandals at the X-way charities, a lot of workers here have been going in and canceling their donations. And rightly so. Why should we give our money to those folks, just so they can pocket it?

<u>Whatever floats your, uh, boat</u>—Why is Eachy hanging around the bathrooms . . . Is he listening to us, do our business? Some people get their kicks in weird ways!

<u>Looking for a big desert</u>—Watch out! Management is opening their chests and letting their hearts fall out. They're providing a roast beef and ham dinner on our lunch hours this Thursday. They must have had leftovers from Christmas. This is for three months of very good production. Well thanks for the dinners guys, but a slice of roast beef doesn't pay the bills. That dinner will repay us for about 10 minutes of those three months of great production we gave to them. Maybe they'll give us a huge doggie bag to fill up and take home with us.

<u>Cleaning break</u>—In the last three months, we surpassed production goals. So our reward was more work. They shut the machines down for about an hour so we could clean them. We're sure we looked busy to the stupervisors. We should take breaks like that more often!

<u>Hang management charts</u>—There are a few more charts management should hang over the vending machines. We want their time spent in the break rooms and the cafeteria smoking and doing nothing, charted. And we want to chart of their <u>real</u> profits. Don't be afraid boys, let your greed show. It's better than a shrink!

BYOC—Open House is May 3, bring your own chairs!

Shocking—It's spring, the roof is leaking and we need to have plastic all over the machines. If you happen to have a puddle on the floor next to an electrical panel, be sure to have your stupervisor stand in it when they turned on the power. That's what stupervisors are for, right?

Musical chairs—Why is management throwing out our chairs in the trash hopper? Didn't we give them a happy face, the last three months, beating their expectations on running production? Apparently nothing we do will convince them to leave our chairs alone. So some workers are wetting down chairs and desks with water in the north break room. Some even took off the wheels on the foreman's chairs. And when the new chairs were brought in, someone cut the seat with a knife. If the supervisors are so mad. They should be mad at the people that give the order to throw out our chairs.

United . . . against the workers—The company wants us to give to the x-way charities. But when it comes to giving time off for absenteeism, or for coming back from breaks late or running a little bit of scrap, there is not a bit of charity in them!!

Hypocritical oath—The nurse is supposed to help people with their injuries and problems, so why is she calling our doctors and trying to talk them out of the restrictions, he gives us? We want a new nurse, not someone who cares more about the Corporation than our health!

<u>Double standard</u>—Mr. Foolproof doesn't run production, but has still managed to run thousands of dollars of scrap parts on the hardness machine. He didn't follow the SOP, and the SOP's are supposed to be foolproof but this fool fell through the safety net. Will he get disciplined for running scrap or is it going to be a double standard as we have seen before?

<u>Give generously</u>—On day shift, we will be taking up a collection soon to buy Eachy a halloween costume. We thought we would buy him a little white tailed deer outfit, complete with antlers and a white tail. Quite appropriate, don't you think for the season?

<u>Rollback stupervision</u>—Hey, plant manager, what happened to all the screaming and crying about sabotage? When things go well, its good management. But when things go bad. It's sabotage, wrong! When things go well. It's all of us working together, but when things go bad. It's management! Sabotage is what management does to the work force on a daily basis.

<u>Smoking problem solved?</u>—The new first-aid engineer has solved the smoking problem in the break rooms. She had suggested that the doors be kept shut, to keep the smoke in. And to build a wall down in the middle of the room. "Where do they find these people"?

<u>Dog chases Rabbit</u>—The Dogs spent most of the morning criticizing Peter Cottontail for not doing his job and says "he doesn't care". But the dogs spent all day sitting in the break room smoking cigarettes with his favorite employees. Not doing his job. The dog caught the rabbit!

"I mean, why <u>not</u> up production? We don't have to work the 12-hours!!"

<u>Don't invite him out</u>—Morale is up a little, and as long as Eachy stays off the shop floor and at his desk.

<u>To be absent, or not to be absent . . . we decide!</u>—A new absentee policy? Maybe. Will it be worse than the last one? Probably. How will the plant managers own absentee record fair compared to the new absentee policy? We think he would be terminated. He's got the worst record in the front office, besides Sleepy Bear. Chilly boy has a good absentee record. You would too, if you only work five days a week, and you didn't have to do anything all day!

<u>Fair warning</u>—Management better watch what they say when they start talking about the women on their shifts. The walls have ears, and it just might be sexual harassment. And we don't take too kindly to that!

<u>Welcome</u>—We'd like to welcome all the workers who were hired just recently. And don't worry if you are new, in a week you'll know more about this place than management ever did!

<u>Nice idea, but . . .</u> —We'd like to enter the quality month poster contest, but we don't have time. We're not sitting around doing nothing, like quality management is!

<u>Or bifocals</u>—Did anyone see the pictures of the four new employees in the front lobby? If you did, you must have had magnifying glasses to see them.

<u>Look before you leap!</u>—Chucky Pease discussed the new policy on absenteeism and some concern was expressed by the Union about the handling of restricted hours. We would express concern that any absentee

policy should and must be applied to all workers, salary and hourly. It will be clear discrimination if it only applies to us.

<u>What's next? Passwords?</u>—Pictures are to be taken for picture Ids on Tuesday. What do they think this place is anyway? Fort Knox?

<u>Loose track of someone?</u>—There is one worker on layoff in the automatics department. Why? They are working daily overtime and weekend overtime in that department.

<u>Stand up and take it like a worm</u>—G.I. Joe didn't know what to do with a recent ISIR, coming off of one of the assembly lines. Doesn't the quality department know what they're doing? Wouldn't it be fun for quality month, for everyone to ask G.I. Joe questions about quality and watch him squirm like a worm?

<u>Drops from the ceiling</u>—Remember the old company birds? Well we know we got the new company birds now. Because it's always dropping its doo-doo on our shoulders! Here is a new game, we can play in their spare time. "Dodge the company bird" if you can run from one end of the plant to the other without getting dropped on, you win!!

<u>Too fast to catch</u>—We workers all want to produce quality parts. But it gets tougher and tougher to catch anything when Eachy drives only for production. Were left letting it go until the end and then sorting them out..Its like counting raindrops in a thunderstorm. Might as well just stick a bucket out and measure the rainfall later.

Another day at the company—Peter Cottontail gave the go-ahead to run the hardener, after he checked the micro-structure. But guess what? We ended up with 7000 pieces of scrap pins. But, doesn't he check the micro-structure in the heat treat every day? And doesn't that leave all parts ran in heat treat in question? We shouldn't worry though, the Plant manager can juggle any scrap numbers!

Freedom from the bull——If management says were responsible and mature, why did they insist on this kind of change to the absentee policy? Why don't they offer incentives to bring people in, rather than clubbing people at the drop of a hat and trying to affect their employment? We know it's not a fair policy. Salary people can take their vacation like sick time, one or two days at a time. Union workers don't have that option. It'll be tough for and lower seniority workers, too, because they can't refuse overtime if they're too tired to work it. Then, if they can't come in, it's an "unscheduled absence". If the company were mature and responsible, they'd leave our absences up to us.

On personal business—Hello, ... bank? There is a new absentee policy at work, I won't be able to pay you until shutdown!

Get a real nurse—The nurse is gone. Guess she won't be asking anyone else to drop their pants anymore. We feel healthier already! But why hasn't she been replaced? Okay, so having no nurse, is better than that nurse. But a real nurse is what we need. And this time, let her do her job, without personnel meddling in.

<u>Misty eyed</u>—Some departments are filled with oil mist. It's easy to see, the mist collectors aren't working. Didn't they promise us that 95% of the oil mist would be gone? It's more like we still have 95% of what we did have. And for that, they told us, no eating on the lines. Yeah, okay, we shouldn't be eating in here and we shouldn't be working in there!!

<u>Get up to date!</u>—When a retiree's wife died recently, he didn't have enough life insurance to cover the funeral. When we retire, the company should at least give us enough life insurance to cover the funeral expenses. We only get $1000 for the retiree only, not the spouse. Where's the company living, back in the 1920s!!

<u>Managements fault</u>—Why do the company Nerds call the absentee policy the "no-fault policy"? Why will we pay a penalty if it's no-fault? They should have named it the "new default absentee policy". A <u>real</u> No fault absentees policy would be nobody gets blamed!

<u>Eachy's big mistake</u>—When a worker challenged Eachy about a chair he wanted to remove from his line, Eachy got angry and went overboard. Eachy just couldn't keep his big round belly out of a pushing match, and discovered that pushing doesn't pay. The plant manager tried to cover the whole thing up by saying it was just an accident and a misunderstanding. It was a misunderstanding all right, Eachy didn't understand how angry workers are getting, about those chairs!

<u>Who configures?</u>—For years line 16 hasn't worked well and it's been running lots of scrap. It's obvious that the machine has needed a complete overall for years. How many thousands of dollars in scrap has it run?

Wouldn't it be cheaper to fix it? Yeah, but leave it to management . . .

Sparks fly!—The year went out with a bang! Almost all second shift and third shift didn't come into work on Tuesday, they voice their displeasure with the new absentee policy. And when management started to run the lines themselves, other people went home. So they tried to move other workers to fill in, and even more workers went home sick. When we went on Christmas vacation, we weren't sick at all!

Faulty numbers—The situation in inspection is getting pretty crazy. Why spend all that time testing bearings, when the testing equipment is itself is unreliable?

We made it happen—There's been all sorts of angry reaction to this new company absentee policy, enough to spur two letters attacking that policy. One anonymous, and one from the bargaining committee. Now the company is saying it's learned something, and they are re—thinking the policy. Well, if they learned something new about the policy, they learned they can't impose it on a bunch of angry workers

Quick action—With all the rain we've had, waters been leaking through the roof like a sieve, all over the plant. So managements getting right on the problem. There is some new crib items, buckets and hoses for ceiling leaks!

Breaking and entering?—Ill-Pill has been breaking into toolboxes. He said he was looking for Jimmy Hoffa . . . but we know better.

Fired!—A worker on midnights was fired recently because he was asked to work second shift on Saturday. He said he had other plans. Of course, he was a probationary worker, so he didn't realize he had to throw his life down at the feet of the company!

Penny wise, dollar foolish—How cold does it get in the assembly room in the winter? Would you believe as low as 64° some days. If management wants better absenteeism, why don't they spend a few dollars on more heat? Or they can lose thousands, when a lot of us are out sick!

Company products are not worth that much!—Remember the ice storm? Many of us didn't show up for work. Were not going to put ourselves at risk, by driving into work on a sheet of ice. Absentee policy or not!

Bad Samaritan policy—There are a number of reasons why the new absentee policy stinks. The ice storm last week was one. There's another, if you witnessed a traffic accident, you couldn't stop to help and get to work on time. The company is always looking to help out other people . . . not

10-4 W3, Get a handle on that tongue—While Ill-Pill was posting up 12 job postings, someone asked if business was picking up. And W3 snapped if people that work here would do their jobs, we wouldn't have to post so many jobs. He's just mad because he had to get out of his cushy chair and do some work. Apparently, there weren't any toolboxes around to work on!

Good doggy, good doggy—The dog had bones put in is a desk, so he could have a after work treat. After that, he had a bone to pick. And he's good at that. Down boy, down boy!

Dr. Scary, cure yourself—Big Scary made it clear where he thinks the problems are. The buck doesn't stop at his desk. But, if you have problems, he'll be glad to listen to it.. It's all in our heads, and he's a therapist. He's got a chair in his office for us, or a couch . . . ?

Big Scary first patient—So many chairs have been thrown out by Eachy, that workers are starting to chain up their chairs so no one can move them. Eachy obviously has a lot of deep-seated hostility towards chairs. Maybe he should talk to Big Scary about "that problem of his".

On-the-job party—Party Animal in one of the new departments must be working on getting a promotion, when he is here that is. And when he is here, he is always in our way. Why do we have to trip over him all day? If he doesn't find something to do soon, we might just have to throw a big party in the break room!

Conserving doughnuts?—When seven salary workers retired recently, the company really saved money on buying donuts, because if all seven would have retired at different times, the company would have to buy seven times the amount of donuts. And if saving that much wasn't enough, they ran out of donuts in the middle of the day shifts celebrating their retirements!

Have a nice day off—Why hasn't the absentee policy been explained yet? How do we know the rules we are to go by? If we are really sick and feel we can't work, should we come to work sick so we won't get fired or written up? Their silence must mean we don't have an absentee policy anymore. Guess that's what they mean by no fault!

Dirty water—Lately, the water from the drinking fountains, has been tasting worse and worse. And the drinking fountains themselves look disgusting, there is a hard crappy build up all over them. And were supposed to drink this water? Isn't the company filtering it or are they trying to poison us? If they're not going to give us clean water, the least they can do is clean the drinking fountains, so we don't have to look at it. And add in some Kool-Aid, so we don't have to taste it!

Radical idea—The company called in all the cafeteria workers, to discuss the quality of the food. What's to discuss? It's not the worker's fault. Just buy decent food, and lower those prices!

To the note—Recently a note went up on the bulletin board that rang true. It's said that we must be second-class citizens in here when management gets fat bonus checks, and we workers get nothing. But how can we all be "in this together", and all be "team members"? Obviously this is a lie!

The bosses ideas vs the workers—They say, can't you see were all in this together. Yeah, right, go tell that to your "conservative friends".

The Left Hook :
Part three

<u>Dummy hyper-man</u>—On second shift, there is a stupervisor, who thinks he has to have his fingers in everyone's machines. We know how to do our jobs, so why does he always have to be messing with us? He's like a hyperactive child that has to be everywhere at once. We think he should lay off all that coffee, and start dipping into his kids ritalin supply!

<u>Rocket Man</u>—Madame Butterfly's prince came to see her recently. We hope no one lets him drive while he was here. One day when he worked at the plant, he drove into the parking lot and had a head-on crash with a light post. Maybe he should get a pilot's license, so he can fly. There is no light posts up there!

<u>They should be accountable</u>—Management thinks all over-time is good for us. We need all overtime to be voluntary only. A good example of how our needs don't always match the companies is when a worker on third shift fell asleep on the way home and ran off the road. It was serious and he was hurt bad. Why does management push us past our limits? Are the companies products worth that much?

"I'd like to deposit my bonus, please..."

Plumbers aren't chemists—The chemist is having the plumbers do the water checks, instead of doing them herself. But she's the chemist, and they are not. She's the qualified person, not them. Who knows what they might be missing in our water? One obvious problem is excessive minerals in the water. That crust is not collecting on the fountains from nowhere. But instead of having the plumbers check on the filtration system, the companies got them testing the water for the chemist. Does that make sense?

You can do better—The stupervisor in the tool-room doesn't treat all of the workers the same way, why? Some workers actually get treated good! This shows us he could be treating all of us better. This is a very small step for mankind, but a giant step for the stupervisor in the tool-room.

Drunk drivers—What does management want? Do they even know? First we go to 12 hours, then were right back down to 10 hours. We go down to six days a week, and just like that, we get behind by 300,000 parts! So, we're right back to seven days a week. Management just stops and starts without reason, we'd hate to be riding in a car with a driver like that!

Good advice—Management has been telling people who've been out one or two days to stay out three days and take a medical. That way, it won't count on your absenteeism. That's a great idea, we should all keep this in mind. Unbelievable, here's is a time where we could actually listen to management.

<u>Now hear this</u>—Management's new policy, take three days off on a medical for any illness. Hey Joe, you feel sick? Yeah, I am going up north, where you go'in?

<u>Management's shop rule book</u>—#1 Just because you have hired us doesn't give you the right to try and run our lives. #2 Don't ask us, what we have been doing all day or all night when you have been sitting at your desk all day or all night. #3 When you do walk by and see us sitting down, don't automatically think we're wasting time. We've worked hard to get the production we do have, so it's not a good idea to piss us off. #4 If you're not going to listen to us, tell us. Don't say, I'll see what I can do, with the intentions of never doing anything. #5 Do not expect us to work every Saturday and Sunday, when you <u>don't</u> and won't.

<u>It got flushed!</u>—The new absentee policy has come to a close. The NLRB has agreed with our union and told the company to blow it off until they negotiate the next labor contract. All that arguing, all that stress, all that wasted time spent on an absentee policy that was unfair, and now it's down the toilet. The personnel director was put out of a job because of an absentee policy. So now he and Chucky Please have failed to force us to accept this same treatment. But don't think it's over, the company spends thousands of dollars a year to have these people make it harder on us. It should show them we can and will defend ourselves!

<u>Dancing fools</u>—Why no radios? It's not in the shop role book. They spent $6-$10000 on a shop rule books, and two days later they have to add to it. How do they explain it? Radios is not in the shop rule book, it's "a plant policy". But the plant policies aren't written down

anywhere. How convenient!. Do they have something against music, or are they afraid they will break out dancing.

<u>Archaeologists will collect their bones</u>—The plant manager told us he hopes to make $1 million by the end of the year. We're all supposed to work harder to help him reach his goal. Mr. Plant manager, do you really think we believe that one? When managers like you don't exist anymore, workers will be given fair treatment and real profit sharing, because we'll be running things. And we won't have to hear the lies to motivate us. But don't feel bad, Mr. Plant manager, we will think of you in the same loving way, we now think of the dinosaurs.

<u>Add this one up</u>—The new absentee policy pushed the absentee rate in the month of January to a new low, .9%. From what management tells us, production should have been higher in January, but it wasn't! Now in March, after we got over the scare tactics and the hype, production was backed up and the absentee rate was back to normal. Now, go figure!

<u>No shutdown?</u>—"I feel a flu coming on". "Yeah, I think it'll hit the first week of July"!

<u>OSHA</u>—OSHA's coming back this week, ha, ha, ha, what a joke. If we want safety around the plant we'd be better off sticking together and protecting each other.

<u>Why don't they tell us their plans?</u>—The company moved some lines out of the plant, but what plans do they have for that empty space? Maybe there planning

to pull a fast one. Contract time is coming up. So maybe they are planning to put something in the there. Anyway, but want to use it as a bargaining chip during the contract negotiations to have us give up something for the new lines.

Strike two, three, you're out!—Production requirements in the new grind will soon increase. The company has proposed a four day work week, 12 hours for three days and six hours for the fourth day. Some of us now work 12 hours a day seven days a week and we get time and a half for Saturday, and double time for all day Sunday. Personnel, you can put that in the same trash can you put the old absentee policy!

Donut sharing—Why doesn't the company buy a bakery? They could get all the free donuts they want to give us. And maybe they could make a few bucks to boot.

In walks the clown—If you get a problem settled between you and your stupervisor, don't let Eachy know the settlement. He'll screw it all up!

Whose lunchtime is it?—Recently three workers on first shift were reprimanded for going outside on their lunch breaks. But just because the company buys our labor they think they can treat us like children. 10 minutes of our lunch is company time, and they don't want us to go outside. But what difference does it make to them, what we'd do in those 10 minutes? Must be someone's on a big ego trip.

Info is coming down the chute—Hyper-man doesn't even wait a minute or two before paging you back to your line. And when you don't answer right away, he pages again. Someone should tell him how long it takes to relieve oneself. If he can't understand, put a telephone in the toilets!

Attention: red alert!—The company hired four more workers last week. Only one was a woman. Contrary to what the company may think, sex has nothing to do with setting up or running machines. By the way, we want to warn the new workers about how fire—happy the company is. Management and some of the brown-noses can be a problem. Now, we said it, don't say we didn't warn you. Until you get your 90 days in, play at cool.

Sound test booth or country club?—Wow!!! What a sound test booth. Wonder how much that set them back? They spared no expense on that one. Walls are four layers thick with chrome and aluminum trim, wow. That must have cost as much as some good houses do. But what the hell, if they have the money, why not spend it. Right? Let's see the same logic at contract time!

Left them cold!—Did it surprise anyone when the new assembly supervisor quit. We could tell right away, she wasn't going to last long. Dedicated to doing her job and one of the nicer, intelligent stupervisors. Guess she was tired of taking crap from the stone-head boys and upper management. She could tell where they're headed and left. Who's next?

Your award, or rather reward—Friday the company will give out awards. We all deserve a lot more than a little pin they hand out. At least make it something useful.

A week extra vacation maybe. They should call them rewards, considering that management wouldn't get their fat paychecks without us!

Bogy'd, this time—Why do some stupervisors seemed so teed off? They are driving hard, but always landing in the rough. Maybe they are playing par too many holes which putts them at a handicap. The least they could do is straighten up and fly right!

It's our business and not theirs—Don't forget when you get a doctor's note, it better include a diagnosis. Management has been making people go back to the doctor if they didn't include a diagnosis on the note. But what business is it of theirs why we were out? If a doctor excuses it, that ought to be enough. What are they looking for, something to hold over our heads?

Take five, outside—Management smokes outside the office doors by personnel. If it's bad for our image to have people hanging outside smoking, what does it say about our image when management does it? Or maybe now they are less image-conscious? Guess that means we can take a break outside now and smoke, right?

A poem—Overtime, overtime go away. Come again another day.
The weekend is coming and we want some fun. So here we go, out for some sun.
When we get back, don't give us a stack,.cause we'll puts you in a gunny sack.
Work, work, work, you know we do. So what we don't need is a boss like you!

QA report—Well, it doesn't look to good out in the plant lately. Why? All 5/8" parts may have cracked ends, all production did stop on two assembly lines. Mass sorting is being done on the magna flux. Customers are sending parts back. And all since Trashman changed the roll process induct-o-heat to save the company money. Well, we can't afford to save any more money!

Management alert—Management says: No "cracking" jokes allow!

Penny wise—There have been a lot of quality problems lately. Cracked end pins, rust and more. Has upper management, been putting pressure on lower management to save some money? If they have, this has led to some bad decisions. They didn't see the quality problems this created until it was too late. They don't know what is going on in the plant. Now they're going to want to stress quality for a while, until they decide to try and save a few more pennies again. If they keep saving money like that, we'll all be out of work.

Take positive action—Quality problems? They don't just happen. So . . . do something useful . . . Eachy, get . . . out . . . of . . . the . . . building . . . now!!!

Running against the wind—Big D has a management style that is close to the stone-head boys. The only difference is, she doesn't have the support group. Like them, she doesn't have to make sense, because she's a stupervisor.

A shrinking violet—If the MOA book was printed the same size as our contract book, it would be bigger. It shows you what they value more. It is been said, and a couple of years you could probably put our contract on the bubble gum wrapper! If we even have one!

We hear them calling—Down the road, a new plant was built, have you seen it? And did you see the jogging and walking trails winding around the plant? Maybe personnel would let us walk down there on our lunch and breaks. Better yet, maybe management will, then we could lock the door on them!

Don't worry, be happy—How many managers does it take to make good parts? . . . None! If you had 10 managers in the workplace, what would you have? . . . 10 too many! How long does it take for a manager to make a decision? . . . He doesn't need to think too long, because he never takes the blame for a bad one!

Company inefficiency—Last week, we all got copies of the MOA, complete with colorful covers. The next day we got a copy of our new contract. Well that was quick. We only agreed to the contract last summer. What did they do, copy them all out my hand? Now we know what they mean when they talk about "efficiency".

The only way—The company really wanted to be sure that we understand the MOA. So they had a meeting at the end of our shifts. But after they were done talking at us, the shift was over. So everyone left without asking any questions. Let's have another meeting, only this time it will start at the beginning of the shift and go until the shift is over, or until we run out of questions. Then everyone one will have plenty of questions.

<u>The company should plan ahead</u>—Hey! Who repairs the toilets? The one in the locker room doesn't work. How long does it take to clear the line? It's been weeks. By now, someone could have gone through an apprenticeship program to become a plumber!

<u>Don't insult us!</u>—The human resources department has been handing out thank you letters for achieving XX amount of years of service, so we can pick out a free gift. Reportedly, a bunch of junk!

<u>Toxic air</u>—The local newspaper had an article that said the company was the sixth highest toxic air emitter in the county, 8560 pounds of toxic waste were put into the air from this plant! And that was just the toxic air that left the plant. The article didn't even mention the toxic air that stayed in the plant. The EPA always talks about cleaning up toxic waste dumps. Well were working in one right here!

<u>Turned themselves in</u>—The information in the article about the toxic waste released into the air comes from the polluters themselves. They are supposed to be honestly telling the government how much poison they dumped into the air . If they use this system for the big companies like our plant, why not for the workers. We could start by writing our own parking tickets. A least that would cut down on the number of tickets.

<u>Purge the desks</u>—We heard top management is supposed to discuss with the stupervisors to see if they would like to have a desk in the front office

instead of the break rooms. We wish you luck, if you asked us we would tell you, they shouldn't have been put in the break rooms in the first place!

Incentive plan—The company explained that new productivity incentive plan to us. Management has always had a plan like this, but apparently they haven't been able to milk it enough, so they want to add our absenteeism in order to improve "their average". They would do the same thing with "their productivity" figures, but they already got them from us anyway.

Goals—The company set the goals for productivity. We don't have any control over them. This would be fine, if it was just managements bonus tied to the these goals. Then it would be more like a wager they make on what we are going to do. But they want to tie our bonus to their goals!

We scream for ice cream—A couple weeks ago, the company gave us free ice cream, and it was good. But we only had it for one day, and so we had to eat as much as we could, and for some, a little more than that. Some people got sick from all the ice cream. The solution to this problem is obvious, free ice cream all the time so that we don't have to eat too much because it's only there for one day!

What is human intelligence?—Reactionaries who defend the system often use the results of IQ tests to say that the inequality in wealth is based on inequalities in intelligence. Wrong! We live in a society of exploitation, not based on intelligence, but instead on force.

Ever increasing goals—We think the company has missed the bus on the new bonus plan. To set a limit on only 5% of our income means it's a negative program. Because if we hit and then go over our goals, we don't get any more bonus, only higher rates the next year.

Heading for the ditch, fast!—Sgt. Brainstorm is messing up all the time on first shift. He goes from one end of the plant to the other making bad decisions. From his very limited knowledge of how to make bearings, he goes around telling us what to do. So, okay, we'll do exactly as he says, and you know where will be!

Sort the scrap out—Have you noticed that management acts like they want to blame us for shipping out bad parts to the customers. Why, if they would have the bad parts sorted out first instead of putting more of a workload on us . . . Must be a part of all the MOA crap they're trying to unload on us.

Egg shells—With the MOA coming up, the stupervisors are walking on eggshells. Do they have a future with a company? Will they have the authority over us they seem to enjoy so much? What if they had to be our equals? Well, you can be sure they have our sympathy!

MOA meeting—There is an MOA meeting coming up in May. We just wanted to know, is that the meeting where we're going to start making the decisions about our work? Company MOA self-help classes? Gee-z, I can't believe we fell for this again.

The fines are a fine?—Anti-dumping laws is enemy number one for the company. It goes against the companies plans to ship more and more parts into this country, the country that buys them. Why? Because it wants to undersell its competitors here in the US, which forces our competitors all out of the business. So the company chooses to pay large tariffs and anti-dumping fines. So don't tell us, the company doesn't make big, big profits. So much so, it can waste it on fines!

Grievances—The bargaining committee said recently that there will be no more grievances. That everything will be settled out on the shop floor. Well, knowing how responsible management has been in the past, this shouldn't be a problem. And of course, we'll probably have to remind them not to decide against themselves on everything that comes up.

Information we need—We had a benefit fair last week with balloons and all the hullabaloo. So when are they going to bring out the clowns from the front office?

Don't get spaced out—Where does all the tramp water go? Where does all the sludge we produce go? Where does all the garbage and the trash go? If they're burning it, it's going up in smoke. If it's going to the landfill it's polluting our ground. It's costing much more than the money the company spends trying to get rid of all this pollution. It's costing us our planet we live on. Maybe that's why the government is trying so hard to travel to outer space!

One hand washes the other—Eachy has been put on quality, on top of already being scrap-master. Now he can decide what should be scrapped. You can bet the numbers on the scrap rate and such will look real good, and the charts will probably be even better. But how will the Bearings look?

<u>More big trips?</u>—The company at MOA committee is off visiting other plants around the country trying to see what MOA is really like. Isn't that funny. They didn't even know what they were doing before it was imposed on us! Sounds more like their followers than leaders.

<u>Remember Q-tips?</u>—Q-tips has come and gone. It was a phase, the company went through. MOA? Just think of it this way, here today, gone tomorrow!

<u>S.O.P.</u>—Definition of MOA : A bunch of wanna-bees.

<u>Jokes</u>—What has the newsletter got to do with MOA? They are positive, it's negative. What do MOA and dirty diapers have in common? They are both full of the shit. What do workers and MOA meetings have in common? One works, the other tries to stay out of it. What do OJ and MOA have in common? They both think they're innocent. Question: What are we going to do about the oil and chemicals from here that are polluting our groundwater around this area? Answer: this is not the type of question you should be asking with the MOA. Just stick to running production, will you?

<u>Snakebite committee</u>—The new MOA Committee is starting now. What do they think they're going to do, change our contract? We don't think they should try, without a vote by the entire membership. They say we make the decisions, but they are telling us how <u>their</u> system works, and how easy we will fit in. So then

they pick who will be on their committee, not us, and again, we are not in control, and it's not a democratic process, is it? We've always said we could run the plant better than management can, so now they're going to let us, right? Wrong! If we ran the plant, the first thing we would do is not have them tell us how to run the plant.

Christmas present—We hear some supervisors didn't get a Christmas present they wanted this year, to be "team leader". Well don't feel bad, you know that if it was up to us, you would have got something nice like . . . an old shoe or a lump of coal.

Wish List—Lots of people here know someone who works at a place where they have had a Modern Operating Agreement.? So what have we heard about them MOA in other places? Well, the company makes sure they get the things on their wish list, like increased productivity, while workers get speedups, job losses, and more injuries. The company wants us to believe that they will look after the things on our wish list and we don't have to worry about it. Yeah, and we believe in Santa Claus too.

Big vote coming up!—Wow! That's real big of the company and the union. Letting us vote on the new plant slogan. Democratically we can vote only because they said we could, now, that's what they think democracy is. We can vote on a slogan, but not on who sits on the MOA committee. Thanks, not!

Buck the system—With the MOA the company thinks we can forget about a safety committee, forget about the fire brigade committee, forget about the social committee and we can forget about our union committee. How can the union buck the system, when they've agreed to it?

Railroad Incorporated—As we go on this big journey with MOA. "Workplace Railroad Inc" only know where we are going, but they want it to be our idea. So they are willing to meet with small groups of us, until a group comes up with an exactly what they want. Then "Railroad Inc". will start firing up the big steam engine and asking everyone to get on board!

Cap salary hiring—So, as we save the company more and more money using their MOA, "Making Obscene Attacks" in the plant. All the while they hire more and more salary workers, engineers and stupervisors. So, we work harder, and they get to work smarter. We don't think so!

Lets get positive!—MOA (Members Opposing Ass kissing) should get organized and start meeting soon. With all this negativism going on, we need some positive influences to talk about. Like how positive we are that we're not going to start kissing ass.

Christmas cheer—Well, Thanksgiving is over and the next thing you know, it'll be Christmas. Getting ready for Christmas takes a lot of time. If the company really wants us to have a happy holiday, then they'll just have to let us have some time off to prepare. Or they could play the part of Scrooge again this year!

A new and improved name—Hey we almost forgot to tell you, T5 should lower the overhead feeders to waist high, so no ladder would be needed. Of course, the company might want to raise the machines up to the automatic feeders, that would make more sense to them!

Top secret—The company is always telling us that they never have any money. They probably tell their customers the same thing, to make them think there getting a good deal. But if that's true, why do they cover up the cost of part components board, whenever a tour comes through? What have they got to hide? Or should we say, how much have they got hide?

Shell game—We hit 100% production for October. People have been wondering what happened to our coffee and doughnuts. Well, the company must have decided that if we want free doughnuts next month. We don't have time for them this month. So, no doughnuts.

Thought for the week—From the company's newsletter, quote, "If you go slow enough, long enough, you'll be in the lead again". Actually, we were counting on it!

Surveys—It's a good thing we filled out those surveys about workplace transformations that we got last year so carefully. Because now every time we don't like something, we're told, but "you said you wanted it". Well, it must be true. In fact, they probably come have some full color charts tucked away somewhere to prove it.

Job openings—Some skilled trades jobs are opening up because people are leaving. The company likes to use the opportunity to divide us against each other, competing for a favor from the company. But the company doesn't do us favors for anyone but the company. If we depend on the company for favors, then they can threaten to take it away later. Anyway, they'll probably just hire their relatives for the jobs, as usual.

It's never too early—Were taking a survey on our own. Has anyone seen Early shut his mouth since he has become a stupervisor? He seems to know how to get out of every tight spot he gets into, at least with his mouth? He's got everyone's attention now, but how long will it last! Early to rise, Early to bed! And then "out the door with Fred".

Earthquake—The new plant manager came on the scene talking about making big changes. It was going to be "fun" again, he said. Well, we have all been waiting for the earthquake that is really going to shake things up, but so far all we've seen are a few tremors. When the earthquake comes, we will know it, we will get weekends off when we want and the nurse will be here to help us with our medical problems, for a start.

Shots—The company was giving flu shots to people who wanted them. The shots are supposed to help people avoid getting the flu. We were wondering, does the company have a shot, we can get to avoid overtime?

Oil leaks—The company went around the plant trying to fix oil leaks. This saves them money on oil and money on cleaning up the oil. But they missed the oil mist that gets in the air. It must not cost them anything to have us mop it up, with our lungs!

"Does this mean he can't work 4 over tomorrow?"

The big ones coming—Chill-Pill put up a letter about how this one thief stole someone's kids candy. We don't agree with stealing and think that the thief should be punished. But the company is the biggest thief of them all. Stealing the surplus value from our labor. Stealing our health. Stealing our weekends and our time away from our families. Who's going to punish you?

Nurse—The new title for the nurse is "Nurse Kevorkian". While she's busy trying to pin the blame for your injuries on you, you could slip right out of this world!

A long way to go—The Union is posting up all this political material, all about the Democrats they support. But when someone puts up a Republican sticker, they tear it down, just like they would if the newsletter people would run candidates. Why? The Union has a big problem with the democracy . . . . and open debate. And of course the International Union won't even let its members, us, vote to elect our Servicing Representatives or the Executive Board.

Safety videos—A worker was injured cutting open boxes a few weeks ago. The company made the worker watch safety videos and take notes all day long. As if it were us that was the safety problem around here and all that's needed is for us to be more careful. Yes, we should be more careful, but the bigger problem is, the conditions the bosses create, unsafe machines with no lockout devices, asking us to climb on machines to clear the lines, oil mist in the air, pushing us for more and more production, and so on. All these things guarantee that workers will be injured here. A lot of careful workers have already been injured. If

Charlie Reed

management really wanted to do something about safety, they could tackle any of these real problems and stop trying to blame us.

Losing popularity—Why just have the bathrooms cleaned when the company has a tour coming? We use them day after day and need them cleaned day after day. It was better when we had a tour coming every day, but it just doesn't happen that way anymore.

Take a nap—We heard a rumor someone is sleeping in the lobby on the off shifts. Sounds like the front office lobby is a good spot. Is there any room for more? If we are tired during work, the company shouldn't have a problem with us resting. It makes us much more safe and efficient, and of course we feel better while were at work.

Put it . . . . in the circular file—Management couldn't wait for the new absentee policy to write one of us up. It shows what a little talk of teamwork does to them. It goes to their heads! And in our files!

China?—"I really don't see how we can continue to do business with anybody who has such a bad history of mistreating their people". "Are you talking about China"? "No . . . . were talking about the company"!

Little lost plant manager—When the plant manager first came to this plant, he went around all chummy, spending time with everyone, doing a little work here and there. When the plant manager tours the plant now, he looks like he wandered in here by accident . . . . and he's trying to find his way out!

Band-Aid Queen—The Band-Aid Queen must have learned her job at some place nobody else has ever studied at. Every time we bring in a note from one of our doctors, she says it means something different from what we or the doctor thought it meant.

Cost cutter—What have they done to the tool crib? The only thing you can find in their is cleaning materials. It looks like they are more interested in cleaning machines then fixing them. Is this management's idea of cost savings? If so, get rid of them and stock the crib!

She's so vain—Sticky fingers must really like reading about herself in the newsletter, as she grabbed a whole collection of them for herself! Hey, Sticky fingers, there's no need to take them from the workers. The newsletter guy would be happy to give you copies going back to number one, for a reasonable fee!

Definition of stress—Stress is that confusion created when someone's mind overrides the desire to choke the living daylights out of some jerk who desperately needs it!

Let's give it to them!—Did you know, the company gives generously to X-way charities and to area schools? We hope they also give to the workers at the plant this time around in our contract. Our union is negotiating and there is supposed to be a give-and-take. But it's more like we give, and they take!

His number is up—Peter Cottontail is on third shift this week and day shift people are so happy. They don't have to put up with his phony kidding around he does.

His kidding is just a front to stab you in the back later.
Peter Cottontail, we have your number.

<u>Another cost saver</u>—Can you believe it, we worked all
week without two stupervisors. We'll suggest it again,
get rid of all of them all, big cost savings! But we know
why we have stupervisors. Who would do Eachy's
dirty work?

<u>Reader response: playing the Eachy game</u>—having
Eachy in the plant is like . . . .

   1—trying to ride a bike without wheels!
   2—trying to grind a part without your coolant on!
   3—as bad as playing lotto with the bonus ball
   4—trying to play baseball and Eachy demanding
      to coach, pitch, catch and play shortstop all at
      the same time!

<u>Roving seniority?</u>—There is a rumor going around
about the company demanding in our contract
something about every department in the plant having
roving setups. There's nothing wrong with that, but
the company wants them to have a super-seniority.
Meaning the company wants to pick someone to be
our helper-trainer, and we can't bump them off their
shift, the company wants them on. What's wrong with
taking seniority workers to be our trainer-helpers?
They are now anyway! It seems like they're trying to
disrupt the seniority system our union has put in place.
Why? Do they want to screw us up as bad as the
system they have to work in?!!

<u>Dingdong, dingdong</u>—Little Loser-reject doesn't make
sense, and she won't let inspection work overtime

during the week, sorting. She must be trying to save money for her department, right? Wrong! After being asked by supervision in production if the inspection department could sort and charge the time to production, Loser-D Bat said no. Why? It's going to take Sigmund Freud to figure that one out!

Peter-Cottontail—What's happening in heat treat lately? Some workers are going on medical leave and one day last week, no one showed up for work on second shift. We can imagine why, it's such a wonderful workplace!

Plant clowns—Eachy is back, and he and Ill-Pill have been roaming the aisles trying to be like the Gestapo, but they're really the Key-stone cops. We work for our pay, but what do they do to justify their pay?

It's up to us—We are going to negotiate our labor agreement early. Who does that favor? Us or them? Whenever we can settle our contract without problems or a strike that's good. As long as we get the things we want and deserve from the company for our work, it's good. But is the company fair when it comes to grievances? When it comes to treating us fair and equal? When it comes to workloads? When it comes to sharing the profits? The answer is no, no, no and no!

Texas—Your union dollars (dues) is at work or at play?

Bad apple . . . . or Eachy—Eachy was on vacation again for two long nice weeks. And how nice was it? The plant ran better, the workers felt better. Even Foreman talked about how better things were without him. We'll get along, but running the plant with him is like running your car on 4 flat tires!

<u>Giving orders is easy</u>—Why a 3 machine workload and plunge grind department? Why does the company thinks all the operators have to do is push a button to run our machines? It's not that easy! But from their desks, inside our break-rooms, anything would be easy!

<u>A foot in the mouth</u>—Big D was caught running around the plant telling how everyone else's quality is bad. Then, suddenly, without warning, a part was found built backwards in her department! And "presto" Big D's mouth was a lot quieter!

<u>Stress</u>—Many of us are getting stressed out on the floor these days. Why? Because we are running tons of scrap and stupervisors are fanatically trying to hide it from Big-Scary. If he found out, their heads would roll, or at least they ought to!

<u>Cross-eyed</u>—Big D's screwed up again! She had workers that work at the north end of the plant sorting bearings out of boxes in assembly. Their policy is that only those workers who sort bearings from boxes are assembly operators or inspectors. And if anyone should know that, that's the big D.!

<u>Playing with numbers?</u>—Management says the production numbers are up quite a bit since they instituted their new system. But management must be playing with the numbers. There is no way they could have gotten such an increase in production by just running machines during breaks and in five minutes

more at the end of the shifts. Guess they'll find out the hard way, what goes around comes around!

Well-ness?—? Management is now doing their health and well-ness appraisals of us. Of course they're making a big show of how concerned they are about are health. They've done surveys and health appraisals of us to find out what were doing wrong, to make ourselves unhealthy. But what about all the things they are doing to us. The stress, the overtime, and all that bad air, we have to breath day after day. They don't need to spend all that money on fancy studies just tell us what we already know!

Attitude problem?—In response to the well-ness studies the company is saying that all the changes we need to make is in our heads. All we need is a positive attitude, and everything will be just wonderful. We think management needs its head looked at. And while they're at it they could make some changes in the plant too!

Run air bearings!—Why does everyone have to do material handling on Sunday? If most of the plant is working, then it makes sense to have enough support department's scheduled to get the work done. If we don't get the stock we need, then we don't have to run our machines!

Cost savings—What do we need G.I. Joe for when we have to show him how to do his work. It shows he doesn't do his job. He tries to change all of the procedures, so he's the only one who knows what's going on, but even that doesn't help!

A real head scratcher—They're putting in a new mesh belt furnace in the heat treat department and adding new jobs. How many jobs, no one knows yet. It should be easy, one more job per shift. But the company doesn't make anything easy, do they?

Illy-Pilly—Recently Ill-Pill has been telling new hires that he was the chairman. As if he was just like us and on our side, now he's the head of personnel. We can imagine what he says . . . . so if you love the company and keep your noses brown, you can be just like me. Boy, how enticing!

It's Pepto Bismol free?—What a way to start a new job, to have to spend all day with Eachy. The only question is, how do they keep their free lunches down?

The Sun never sets on KD rings—What the hell, bring in another truckload of KD rings. It's just, just-in-time delivery, just in time to collect dust!!

Are you Lonesome tonight?—Why are they hiring more foremans? Are they lonesome and bored in the break room's?

One down, more to go—Did anyone notice the plant running better since the plant manager left for Japan? We did!!

Who's stealing from who?—Half Baked, got burned at the edges of this week. She says workers are taking too long on breaks. She says this is stealing from the company. Well, Ms. Half-Baked, just as soon as the company pays us back for all the profits they made off of our work, then we'll worry about the few pennies they didn't get to steal!

<u>Crawled out from under the rock</u>—Chuck Smock, the corporate blankety-blank paid us a visit last week. Someone must have told him there were free coffee and doughnuts.

<u>The rich man's way</u>—The president of X. Charities has resigned. He only got $463,000 per year plus expenses and were eating hot dogs to raise money for that group?!

<u>To bad it's not true</u>—An inspector was moved out of automatic machines, and he and his coworkers weren't too happy about it. It's just like management to see a group of workers who work well together and split them up. Ms Air Head said it's because he was working too hard. Sure he was, we all are! But when did the company start caring when we do too much, and try to help us do less?

<u>We be Ill— on the Pill</u>—The fumes and mist coming up from the grate, fouling the air, and we just ate! So when the urge arises just call for a Pill, and hope he's just in time for you to get ill!

<u>Unfair treatment</u>—What does management have against women? Seems like any time a Woman worker so much as sneezes the wrong way, some managers starts hollering. They are convinced we can do the job, and they are itching to prove it. They ought to be more concerned about the jobs <u>they</u> can't do, and let us do ours.

<u>Picked but nothing heard</u>—Remember all the way back to November, when it was quality month, and the management picked their plant slogan for the next year. Why haven't we heard anything about it? Something is just not right, we normally have it all over the walls and put in their newsletter and have it splashed all over!

<u>The right decision</u>—Yet another supervisor this week decided to come back to hourly. A lot of them must be getting tired of being under Eachy's gun. Especially when Eachy, hands them a list of jobs to do every morning, <u>his jobs</u>, then goes and smoke cigarettes in the cafeteria. Guess Eachy will have to do his own work for a change.

<u>You get what you give. That's all!</u>—When the company schedules us to work 12 or 10 hours a day, and we don't come in until the regular shift starts, should we be sent home because we are more than an hour late? We would say, no. Why? Well, first because we made the effort to come to work to do a days work for the company. Second, the intent of the contract was if the company put someone in your job and you were more than an hour late, management didn't want to move that person off your job or send him home because he volunteered to stay over 4 hours. Recently, Peter Cottontail sent someone home because he said he was four hours late. We think eight hours a day of work, made more sense than zero hours!

<u>Take a chill Pill</u>—When one of our customers called about some damaged bearings last week, management hit the panic button, running around getting everybody worked up trying to figure out what went wrong and

how they were going to cover their butts on this one. Wouldn't you know it the customer calls back and says it was their fault. Management could have waited just a second before they panicked, and disrupted our day. Now were so worked up, will have to take an extra break, or we might start making bad parts, accidentally of course!

How management thinks—Management showed their priorities when they put out the money for a new roller machine to meet their production needs. But they still haven't done anything about the oil mist collectors that aren't working. It's only our lungs, right?
Well, they have their priorities, and we have ours. The air quality in the cafeteria sure is a lot better than in the north end of the plant.

Stupervisor Phil—The little dictator Phil is telling everyone not to leave their work areas until 11 p.m., and he's trying to hold us to the minute on breaks and lunches. Sorry, Phil, you can't watch us all at the same time. There's too many of us. As a matter of fact, we see you sitting in the break room jawboning your days away. We thought little GD dictators were supposed to set the example. Okay, fine, we'll do what stupervisor Phil does!

Get our checks early!—We have SOP's all over the plant that tell us what and how to do our jobs. Even SOP's that tells us how to lay our shop towels out. Instead of throwing them in the dirty towel containers. We need an SOP for stupervisors, they all go by their own rules. If they can make the rules for us, we should be able to make the rules for them!

<u>We work for it, they didn't</u>—This week we get our 1% checks and the extra money is needed and nice. But why aren't we getting anything from profit-sharing? We worked hard to produce that profit, so why does management take all the profit for themselves? There is something wrong with profit-sharing and that is, why are we sharing the profits with them, anyway?

<u>Let Eachy jump up</u>—The grease alarm in the assembly room is so loud it sounds like an ambulance siren. Boy, they sure can scream when the product might be damaged. Now all we need is a siren that we can set off when things get unsafe for us. And we need to put it right over Eachy's desk!!

<u>Hocus-pocus</u>—Ever notice how the engineers try to fix the machines that's having problems? We can just hear them saying, "if we get enough of us to stand around this machine and talk, maybe the machine will fix itself"!

<u>Not our problem</u>—The boxes for the time-cards are way too small, it's hard to jam the cards into the slots without messing them up. Management doesn't like this, so let management straighten the cards. They should purchase smaller time-cards, or they could get bigger boxes. Either way, it's their problem, not ours!

<u>Pleasant nightmares, Ms. Air-head</u>—Oh where oh where has Little Ms Air Head gone, oh where oh where can she be? With her hair so gray and her eyes so red, oh where oh where can she be? Did she lose her mind because she was so blind, oh where oh where can she be? But while she's gone, we'll sort all day long, right here is where we'll be.

A real cola—Wow! The company gave us a five cent COLA and a $.15 raise. Well let's see, if we work 40 hours a week, we could earn eight dollars more a week. Enough to take a friend to McDonald's for a light lunch, or maybe a snack. Seems like the cost of living has gone up more than that.

Direct ignorance—Some of us wanted direct deposit of our paychecks to the bank, but Chucky Please says we can't. He says they need two days to process the book work but Tuesday to Friday is three days. And if we had direct deposit, second shift wouldn't need their checks on Thursday, the money would be in the bank on Friday! The biggest benefit is the convenience factor, but the convenience and the common sense is not a part of Chucky Please or the company.

Vote— participate—act—We have union elections today and everyone should vote. But our future is not based on who wins or loses. It's based on all of us participating in our union and acting together for our mutual benefit.

Their mistake again—We heard one of the Japanese engineers has always wanted to be written about in the newsletter. He's been around here longer than the newsletter has, five years, and still hasn't appeared. If you wonder why, ask the people that work around him. Management shouldn't be sending him back to Japan, as they are soon. Why not have him be the head of personnel? He would be a person we have confidence in.

"Golly, you have been so good to us this year, running all that production and all. We want to give you a x-mas gift this year. We're going to actually honor the labor agreement for the month of January!"

"Wow! Now we know how you got your name! ILL BILL."

Behind 100,000 bearings?—On Saturdays, we normally run better production and the only difference is, there is not as many stupervisors. Every day should be Saturday!!

Healthy profits or healthy people?—The US spends more money on health care than any other country in the world. But instead of having the healthiest people, we have the wealthiest healthcare corporations.

Acting? the fool—Why do stupervisors pass bad parts down the lines? Because it makes them look better if we keep running their crappy parts and the numbers are bigger. They can always act stupid, if someone finds them later, because they are not acting!!

You maybe next—It seems there are changes in heat treat now. The micro-structure check will be done by the operators now. This will mean more work for us and may be the first step in the elimination of some metallurgists jobs. If so, it wouldn't be new. Workers all over have lost jobs to this kind of speed up and job combination. And it will continue until we come together to stop it.

Stupervisor Filly—Second shift has a little dictator for a general foreman now. What we want to know is what happened to the supervisor we knew? It seems he's gone over to the enemy. When he was on the shop floor, he went behind the butler building with the rest of the guys. Now he hangs out with management, rubbing elbows and has the attitude to match. Well, we've dealt with little F dictators before.

<u>Good attitudes</u>—We have analyzed statements by the Japanese government leaders lately and have come up with some reasons why they feel the way they do. Maybe when Japanese workers are sent to the US to work for awhile and then go back to Japan, they are saying things like, I'm not running 16 machines anymore, I'm running three machines like the Americans do. Or, I'm not mopping up that oil, that's the janitor's job, not mine! Or, run it anyway, management doesn't give a shit. But that's not lazy or stupid. It's smart. Japanese management probably is upset by talk like that. American management sure is. But then again, who cares what the upper crust likes, in Japan over here?

<u>The Dead Rat-man-way</u>—Management is bad, real bad, but there was one plant manager that did his job the way it should have been done, Dead Rat-man. We never saw him. He must have stayed in his corner. If all the managers followed his example, we could fix all of their mistakes and get the plant turned around again in no time.

<u>Donuts and coffee, donuts and coffee</u>—Donuts we get, turkeys we don't. Coffee we get, cokes we don't. Seems like someone up front likes donuts and coffee. Whenever they think to give us something for a job well done, it's always coffee and donuts. Is that all they like, or is that the cheapest reward they can think of? Hey, plant manager maybe you should join donut-aholics anonymous.

<u>No room at the top?</u>—Recently, a probationary janitor was fired for making racist remarks. So why did they

fire him this time? They usually promote someone like that in to management!

Our stomachs aren't that strong—Management must wonder why workers don't anticipate in action teams or problem-solving committees. We don't and we know exactly why. It would mean we would have to work with Eachy and Tree-top. Working with them is about as pleasant as getting the stomach flu!

Top management rule book—#1 don't make too much trouble for us, we will be here a lot longer than you. Special attention for personnel. #2 talk to us right. If you don't talk to your mother that way, don't talk to us that way! #3 don't make up the rules as you go along. #4 engineering, do not try and do our work. We know you don't have a job of your own, but we can do the job a lot better without you in our way.#5 do not give us hot jobs just to get us to do it now and then let it sit after we do it for a week.#6 don't bother us when we stop and talk a while, we have over 30 years to do in this place and five minutes won't break the bank.

Nursery rhyme—The company has a nurse. All she does is make it worse. When you're injured and need attention, she bad mouths you and gives a detention. Workers need to know when their ill, they need a nurse who's not a pill. Nurse, we know you went to school, so work with us. Don't be a fool!

Hands down!—Why are the green aisles oily lately? We have seen people walking along and have one leg come out from under them. How many times do we have to tell management, we need clean floors? We have learned to walk slow. But it's fun to see upper management walking fast, and slip. Maybe they can learn the hard way!

<u>Slow it down!</u>—Quality in the plant has gotten so bad that the Beast and the Party Animal are getting into fights. One says we need better quality, and the other says the machines can't run any better quality. We think they're both right. Slow down the machines, so we can run better quality!

<u>Their a problem? We're too smart!</u>—With all the screening process management put workers through, before they hire us in here, they are still complaining about attendance problems. Could it possibly be that problem isn't the individual worker? Then it comes down to it, they're screening process won't help. Because all workers are the same, if you work the hell out of us, we're going to take a break when we need it.

<u>Someone call a meeting, quick!</u>—With all the oil mist and humidity in the north end of the plant, the company should be charged with attempted murder. To demand that we work in that environment should be against the law. The company has eliminated most of our windows and demands that we not leave doors open. With this much grinding and machining going on in the north end the oil mist it creates, the potential health risk is catastrophic. The company should carry all of the responsibility for what they know they are doing! It's a wonder that they can sleep at night!

The last chapter

We tried to write our own newsletter. But it took us three months to put together and a coworker was working with me, and we had got permission from the Union to do the newsletter. We submitted it to the Vice President of the Union and we waited and waited and the newsletter never came out. And I finally asked the vice president, which I gave the newsletter to for printing and he told me he'd never submitted it. And so we had a little discussion around that, and of course I didn't have the power to force him to do it. So the newsletter went down. So one day I went to a political rally and a guy asked as I was going in, if I wanted to sign a petition for a "workers against concession party". So I said sure, and so we had a little conversation, he said, well, maybe I can call you later and to discuss it, maybe if you want to work on this. A couple days later gave me a call we had a discussion about "workers against concessions party" and running candidates. So, I was picked to run as a state representative, and they had a whole slate of candidates running. So we did that. And of course we never thought we would win. We didn't have any visions of really winning but wanted to get our message across. And so I went to political rallies, and

I spoke at a college and I spoke at a Township Hall for the "workers against concessions party" candidates. We went to county fairs, handed out flyers, and we'd be kicked out of the county fairs because you couldn't hand out political flyers there .But then we discussed having newsletters in the plants and it sounded really good to me. So, I was helping them with ideas of what to put in the newsletter and we started putting it together. They would hand it out in the front of the parking lot as people drove into work. And I would take a few in and put them around the plant and in the cafeteria and break rooms, bathrooms, and in some workplaces, where people would pick them up. They were gold color, so coworkers knew exactly what they were when they saw them on the tables. And we did that for about five years, until people decided to stop and I could see that and I suspicioned that to begin with, that it was a government sponsored program or what ever, I didn't know what it was. This is why I call my book, The left hook, the government (the phony left group, Spark) was giving me the left hook, the company was giving me the left hook and the union was giving me the left hook. But I knew how to fight and was giving them the right and the left! And I was proud to do it. I could see they were run in cells and one cell didn't know what the other cell was doing except they seem to have a worker in the cell, helping write the newsletters. I believe these organizations were set up to neutralize workers like me. They did it slowly all the while trying to find out as much information from me as possible, I found out later every one had fake names except the workers in the cells. Big clue. It wasn't a big worry, it was a way to intervene for my coworker's. I found out for sure by telling three big lies to them. Very big lies, I thought for a long time, and

170

planned what I was going to tell them. The company knew every detail and within a day and a half and the company did react. Let me tell you one. I told them a story that this guy and had a certain shim that he had made up that he could get into any of the offices in the front offices, because at that point nobody in the front offices was working there on the off shifts, I told them that you could dance on their desks up front, and no one would know. And this guy was so neat and clean, I knew he wouldn't have the nerve to do it and no one in the plant could even think that he could. What the company did was, within a day and a half have engineers moved to the off shifts to sit at their desks and do their work. And I could hear them talk, when I walked through the offices. "Why are we having to do this". "I don't understand",but I did. So the second big lie I told them was, they always wanted to make copies of the newsletters. So I told them what the company just got a fantastic new copy machine. And if somebody would pull up to the front door outside the front offices I can roll it out to them. And we could take it and they could have a new copy machine, so within a day and a half. They had a contractor come in and I see them at the front office to get the front lobby completely remodeled. The front lobby people would come into the business and made the doorway much smaller and much more secure and the only way you can get the copy machine in and out at that point is go all the way through the cafeteria all way out to the side doors. So I knew why they had done that. So their reaction told me things, things that no one else knew except me The third big lie was, that I carried a gun into the plant every day and put it in my locker. Now, I knew they'd reacted to that lie. So they started looking in lunch boxes, everybody had to open their lunch boxes as they came in and had the security guard look as people went to the gate and then they went through everybody's lockers, while nobody knew why they were doing that. But I did, and so I got tired of doing the newsletter, and of course I got tired of having the company knowing what we were doing and how we were going to do it, so I quit it. But I knew something had to be done. And of course when you speak truth to power. You have to be very careful and do it anonymously as you can, but we needed help, and the newsletter served the purpose. Otherwise I wouldn't have got to retirement.

So let me tell you about some of the other successes we had. Oliver called me on the phone from outside the plant into the QA office where I worked. The company had terminated Oliver, because he was in jail and on a sick leave of absence, what happened was he was on probation, and was spotted in front of a bar and he was afraid he would go to jail so he went to the doctor got a restriction. Went on sickness and accident but someone pushed an article about that from the local newspaper under the personnel office door. We had people that would do that type of thing. And that's how they found out he was in jail and they terminated him. So he was telling me all about it but the first thing I ask a person when they want help is, are you going to listen to me and do what I ask you to do. Oliver said no problem. So, we continued talking and I found out what I needed to know, everything about the situation, so I could analyze it and tell him where to go first. So before we got off the phone I ask what he doing that afternoon, and Oliver said, I'm just babysitting the kids. I said I want you to go to the unemployment office right now and he said they are not going to give me unemployment, because the company fired me. . I said, Oliver. I asked you when we started this conversation. Are you going to do what I ask and you said yes. He said okay, I'll go get the kids ready and we will go up to the unemployment office and apply. So the next day he called me again and says you will not believe it, they gave me my unemployment. He said but they gave me twice the length of time because the company terminated me when I was on sickness and accident. I said, that's good. So now we have the family taking care of, now we can work on your job. So I said, the first thing you need to do is get into the plant, and file a grievance. I said and make sure you ask him for a copy of it. So you can have it for your records, he said okay in the next few days he was in the plant and he filed a grievance. But he said they told him that it probably wouldn't go anywhere and they probably would have to throw it out. So when he told me that I said go back and tell them they can't throw it out, a determination has to be made up at the international level. And they have to take it to arbitration, so a week or two later he comes back and he said to me that the Union doesn't have enough money for arbitration. I said go back and tell them that they have enough money to take trips to California with their wives. They better have enough money to take people to arbitration, because that's their jobs and it's in the contract. It was funny, I knew within minutes of what was happening in the meetings, in the union office. Because he would call me from outside the plant, just outside the plant in his car. So he came in a few days later and said I think I'm going to file a civil rights complaint. That's okay with me if you think that the company fired you because your black. I said Oliver, tell me what they have said to you that tells you they violated your civil rights. Oliver said

I can't tell you anything, except they fired me and I'm black I said then. We're not complaining to civil rights because that's a dead-end street, okay?. We can use that as our last effort. I'll work with you, you have a good case, so the international came in and said we don't know if this can go to arbitration, and he came back and told me that. And I told Oliver to tell them it's up to the membership. They need to hold a meeting and have a membership vote his grievance up or down on taking your grievance to arbitration. So he did, and they scheduled a meeting and I told Oliver. Don't say anything about you and me working together on this termination or they would get mad, and not help you. And because they'll be a bit pissed, and will get more people to vote your grievance down. I told Oliver make sure you go to the meeting. And when they open the floor up for discussions. I said get up and tell your side of the story and make sure that they know that you applied and got unemployment. So he went to the meeting, and he got up and spoke, told his side of the story and he got a positive response from the membership and they voted in his favor to take his to grievance arbitration. I think it was six or nine months before the arbitrator heard it and he went up there with the union and told his side of the story and the arbitrator ruled in his favor. Giving him back pay. I think it was over $30,000 in back pay and gave him his job back. And he called me on the phone and he said, we won and it was great. He said, I told them you'd been working with me all the time. He said that its too late to go back now, the arbitrator has ruled and he had the report in his hand but I said, no. It's never too late, and what happened was the international rep called to the arbitrator, as I found out later, he told him they didn't want back pay, just Oliver"s job back. So he lost a lot of money because he didn't do what I ask him to do. And that is to keep me out of it. But at least we won his job back. And we were happy about that.

The another good success is much easier to explain. I was eating lunch in the cafeteria and one day, when Al sat down at the same table, and as we started eating our lunches. He was telling me that he wished he could retire so he and his wife could both travel around in there motor-home. I ask him what was the problem, how many years did he have and he said I have 29 years. But if he would get back the other year that I had when I first started. I have would have 30 years and I could retire. He told me that he worked the first year, and then he quit Friday and then they called them back in to work and he said okay and he came back in on Monday. So I said Al go into the personnel office and tell them that under the "Barr-Lee law" you have a right to pick up that one year when you retire, he said you're kidding. So tell them exactly what I said, and then come back and tell me what they told you. I don't even think he finished his lunch. Well the next thing I know they're scheduling a retirement party in the cafeteria for Al. At the retirement party, a younger employee was telling Al about how tired he was and someone overheard Al tell a younger employee that if he goes home tired it's was his own fault. So we made up "Al's rules on work".and posted around the plant. Rule number one is, if you leave work tired, it's your own fault!!. Rule number two, if you see something that needs to be done, have the boss get somebody on it!!. Rule number three, if the boss asks you to do something, find another lower seniority person and tell them to do it!!! We knew Al lived by these rules every day, and it's what got him through. Sadly though, Al died of cancer a year later, but at least he got a piece of retirement thank God for that.

When I was on the safety committee. I would turn in about 10 or 12 problems that we would see out of the shop floor. And when I went to the meetings, I would turn them in, and we would discuss them all and the company would tell us how they would resolve them. I would argue with the company about putting safety rails up at the truck well. At the time, they only have had a small safety chain, which if a hi-low ran into, they would go down into the truck well, and possibly hurt themselves. Sadly after I retired a couple years, I heard someone ran in to that truck well and fell in it with the hi-low and was killed. Of course OSHA found that the company was not at fault. What a joke.

A funny thing happened before I retired was. The company was giving out gifts for a reward. If you worked five years, 10 years. 20 years 25 years 30 years. So I looked at the selection, and I knew they would be handing them out in the cafeteria. The plant manager would hand them out, so I picked out the largest gift I could, and it would come in a box and that was a world globe. So they held the meeting to hand them all out, and I saw my box sitting there. It was huge, at the end of the table. So they started handing out the boxes. It was watches, pins etc. in small boxes. The plant manager went through every one except me. The big box at the end of the table and then he finally got to it. I walked up there and took my huge box and I know everybody was asking and looking at what was it that I got that was that big, I loved it. I knew the plant manager knew about the newsletters, but he had to hand me the largest gift that was passed out that evening.

There was a union steward on third shift you might call him tough, or hard-nosed but I would call him good. We worked for years on different problems, and he never looked the other way and he would always give the bosses a hard time. He would explain things this way, if the company can buy color TVs. At least, we the workers could buy black-and-white TVs. There were serious double standards in the plant, and after years of looking at it and was told by one supervisor, that the plant was mob owned and run, I was starting to believe it. While I don't really know about that, but I do know some of the people they treated decently and give second chances and there were people who used drugs. One person could get caught sleeping on the job and not be fired. Another person could be caught sleeping on the job and would be walked out of the plant. Throughout my working life at the factory. I never could really figure this out. I only assumed the company had special people that they wanted to keep no matter what they did. And so when the company came against somebody and the coworker asked me to intervene for them. I would, I feel knowledge is king. To illustrate that, I looked at what workers needed and some of the biggest problems were Worker's Compensation related. So I saw in a union magazine. They had little booklets for sale for $.25 apiece that explained workers rights and the law. So I ordered 25 and brought them into the plant. When I started handing them out in the plant, they lasted about 20 minutes and I had about 20 other people wanting them. So I ordered 50 more, and handed them out and they went in about an hour and a half. Of course, the company didn't like it, but the people needed to know their rights, and I was seeing to it. One of my coworkers told me they were having trouble getting their workers comp from a company and he asked for help. So I took him up to the personnel office and told the woman working there at the time that we would be camping out on the front lawn by the weekend and would be calling the news papers to tell them. The company wasn't being fair to a Vietnam vet by not giving him his workman's comp and that he was being kicked out at his apartment.. They knew, I meant what I said, so she opened the middle drawer on her desk and pulled out his check and handed it to him. She had it all the time, that's the way the company did business back then, we were always forced to make a fight.

The company was cheating the insurance company, our S&A coverage, by putting people that were supposed to be on workman's comp on S&A for six months until they settled their cases. At that point the company would subtract there S&A from their workman's comp, and give them a settlement check. The problem was, they never went back and re-paid the S&A insurance. The workers had to pay taxes on that six months of S&A because it was taxable, the workman's comp was not. One of my coworkers was complaining about he had to pay the taxes. And I found out the story by him. And someone wrote a little letter to the insurance company, loss prevention. And guess what, we had another S&A, insurance company covering us after that.

One day I was sitting in the QA lab talking to a coworker when another coworker came in. A person that had opposing views than I did sat down and started making nice talk to me. Of course I knew she may have an ulterior motive, and she did tell me something that she wasn't doing as a part of her job that she was supposed to be doing. And I knew she wanted me to tell her something I wasn't doing. So I obliged and told her that I just check off the mainsheet. I don't do any of the other work or submit the paperwork for the line checks. Then we went on talking afterwards, my friend asked me why did I tell her that. I said, because it won't be long. She'll be telling the stupervisor on me and he said you've got to be kidding me. I said no watch and see. So the next day we came in, and here she comes with the stupervisor and told me he wanted to talk to me. So I went out there in the plant, he asked where is the line checks? You were supposed to be doing yesterday I couldn't find them. I saw them digging through the files, and I thought, here we go. So I went out there where the files were and grabbed the line check that I put in line 15 instead of 16, and then put it in the file 16 and showed the stupervisor as he was already walking back into the offices, he new that it was a set-up. They looked like fools, and they acted like fools.

I found out after working years in inspection department, that some of the inspectors would punch in for work and run from their work all day. One inspector, in particular, when we set up a sort on our shift. She would come in, and reorganize the whole sorting process. So she didn't have to do any sorting, she would do this on every sort, reorganize everything to make it look like she had done something, or they had done something and then play all day. I believe the company knew what was going on but didn't do anything. Why I'll never know now.

One time I went on a trip to another plant, with my supervisor, and the quality manager. We took a flight to another state, and then rented a car and drove to the plant. On the way home we stopped to fill the car up with fuel before we dropped it off. I had left the car to go into the store to buy something and on the way back. I saw the quality manager, putting fuel into the car and the supervisor was rolling in laughter in the backseat. I ask him why he was laughing and he said. The quality manager was trying to put diesel in the gasoline fuel car and somebody hollered over to him. Hey buddy is that a diesel. So he quickly put the diesel nozzle back in and grabbed the gas nozzle. Of course this was after the plant manager had given the plant we visited hell for not paying attention to quality. So we joked about it for months afterwards telling each other. "Hey buddy is that a diesel".

The company tried to fire me one time because I took a suspended employee to an open house to the tech lab. While I talk to him about how we could get him back to work. The coworker wasn't supposed to be in the plant, while he was suspended. But the open house was in a different location in the tech lab not on plant property. The next day, the chairman of the Union came and got me for a meeting with the head of personnel, during the meeting, they told me they were going to fire me. And that I shouldn't have taken the suspended employee anywhere on company property, but I told them it was an open house and with an open house, anybody can come. Personnel said it wasn't an open house. It was only for employees only. I told them yes it was. That's what my supervisor said it was. I said let's go ask him so all three of us went walking down the aisle like bulls in the china shop, and my supervisor says, oh my what's this about. I said the announcement, you told us yesterday. He said, you mean the "open house". I said, thank you and I went on back to work.

People were complaining that the water in the cafeteria tasted bad. The people that manage the vending machines came in and cleaned, but it didn't do any good. So I went in to investigate, and I found the drinking fountain in the cafeteria tasted all right. So I got in the back room of the cafeteria and looked at their filter, which they have a large water filter hanging on the wall with a clear glass around the filter. It was as green as your front lawn in the spring time. So again I asked the company to have it changed, and they moaned and groaned, and then never did it. So I call the state health Department and asked them what I could do about it. They told me, if they called the company it would be like hitting an ant with a huge mallet. I said, sometimes they need that. So we decided I could call the county health department, and they would take action for us. So as usual, we got the filters changed, and they changed the drinking fountains filters also. The plumbers didn't like me very much, but everyone else did.

I used to complain to OSHA and EPA and the health department, and whoever else would listen. I called OSHA in about the warehouse furnace one day. A salary employee had asked me to try to do something about it, because she'd went to the doctor and he had tested her blood and said she had carbon monoxide poisoning. So we called OSHA, and OSHA called the plant to made an appointment to come in and test the air quality in the warehouse. Before OHSA came in however, the stupervisors in the warehouse, opened both large service doors and all the windows. When the OHSA inspector arrived we went out to the warehouse stood in the middle, and he did his air quality test. I told him we might as well be standing out in the middle of the parking lot. At that point, he ended his test, and we walked back to the plant. The next day, the company had furnace people come in and tell us that the gas was staying on 30 seconds before the igniter lite the furnace. So, gas was escaping into the atmosphere affecting the workers there. That's all the company had to do, but it always chose to fight us, instead of cooperating.

And there were many pranksters in the plant also. They would put a woodchip in the drinking fountains. So when you pushed to turn on the water, it would shoot 30 feet in the air, and possibly go on your face, then you'd hear them laugh. One day I walked into the break room and looked in the Foreman's desk for something to write with. And every drawer was filled up with T-bone steak bones. I don't know where they got that many bones, but I got out of there quick. Another serious prank happened in the assembly. When I walked in there. I was told I could have some brownies. When I went over to the plate that was by the supervisors deck they told me, no, those are for the supervisors only. Those brownies had ex-lax mixed in. It was harsh, and it sent the supervisor home, but that's the kind of pranks people played.

I'm for workers rights and the Union but there are people that hold union office that shouldn't, and I'll explain. The company transferred, a husband and wife team from another state to our plant. The husband was a supervisor on the shop floor. The wife was head of personnel and kind of nice looking. It was about six months or year that went by, and her husband was transferred up to corporate office. He couldn't take the shop floor and what people would say to him about his wife. But we didn't think too much of it. One day, on a Sunday, she came in early, it was six o'clock in the morning. It was unusual. Later that day we heard something big was up at corporate offices, but they couldn't say but later we found out that he, the supervisor committed suicide in the bathroom. He shot himself twice in the stomach, unusual. So we didn't know why and asked a lot of questions, but no one would say why. We knew that they may be getting a divorce and the stress of that did him in. But we sympathized with her, the head of personnel. They would have his funeral back in the other state he came from. Then we heard all of the Union was going to his funeral. And that was unusual, so people were asking me what was going on, but let's wait and see I said, then let's ask people that go and come back if they'll tell us any information. I asked them to ask the people that went to the funeral. What happened right after the services was all over, and he was buried, and they told me the personnel women gave the chairman of our union, her keys to drive her car back to our state. Big clue, but they still were denying it. And so months went by, a few months, and people came up and asked me what can we do. I told them if they got me some film of the two outside of the plant together that I would take it to the president of the company and see what he would do. I already contacted the international Union and told them there was an inappropriate relationship going on, and company and the union was involved, but they wouldn't do anything. So those young folks got a film of them coming out of their apartment house with her hair wet and them holding hands at six o'clock in the morning and if you turned the sound up loud enough, you could hear them that was filming say look it them, oh my God! So I took that film, and I wrote about 10 things that it violated and it would cause legal problems for the company in the future. If they didn't do anything about it. So I called the president of the company, and he said, put it in an envelope, taped it and staple it and wrap it up and give it only to a certain lady in the office building he was in so, I did. It took about six weeks before the president reacted. I was about ready to move on to some other place to complain about it when they fired her. For lying to the president because he had sat down with them and asked them if they were having a relationship, tapes don't lie. And to make a long story short, they were married within a year. It's hard to believe that the chairman was a pallbearer to the man that shot himself and was married to the head of personnel and later he married his wife! I could go on about the union, but they were a sick bunch. When I was on the bargaining committee. We were sitting in the office and the company lawyer stop by the doorway. He was angry that the bargaining committee was asking for a quarter back that the company owed us. The company, a few days before had taken out the bargaining committee to a fancy restaurant. I declined the go, because I felt if the company was not resolving problems, I don't want to go have dinner with them, the lawyer said as he was standing in the doorway. You know the envelopes that we gave you, while at dinner you would go to prison, if anybody found out. Nobody said a word. They looked like they were scared out of their minds. I asked one bargaining committee member later, what he meant by that and he said, I don't know the lawyer always just talks like that. I always wondered, because previously people would say when they came up to bargaining for the contracts. All of the bargaining committee got new trucks, to me it wasn't a joke.

When I first started at the company. The plant was producing about 100,000 bearings a month. when I retired, the plant was producing 100,000 bearings a day. That's about 3 million or more of a month. I think the company had enough dollars to share with the employees. But I was more concerned with the mistreatment of people. The discrimination, the unjust behavior. The kicking people when they were down, and I worked on it all my working life, I had some failures, but I have a lot of success. One day, while I was auditing parts in assembly I ran across one bearing that wouldn't turn and as I looked into it further I noticed there was a small piece of retainer broken off, blocking the way of the balls. So I went and told my supervisor, and they investigated the line that was running the Bearing and found a small hill of pieces of retainer that was breaking off in the production process. So they hit the panic button, stopped the line, pulled all the parts from the warehouse, called the customer and pulled all parts from the customer and sorted everything. So the rest of the day, office people and engineers would come out and thank me for finding the bad part. So I got to talking to one of the Japanese engineers, and he told me. If we wouldn't have found it. It would cause a million-dollar lawsuit, and he said that company would be gone. And I said, the plant would be gone, he said yes gone!! Me and a coworker decided to have a raffle, a 50-50 raffle to help raise money for people that were off on S&A or laid off. It was a Christmas raffle, and we sold the first year, about $2000 worth of tickets and $1000 would go to the people that were off work. We had $1000 in prizes. First prize was $500, second and third prizes were $250 apiece. It increased through the years so much so that the company took it over, the Christmas raffle was even made it bigger. So we would give half of it to the charities and half of it would go for prizes.

Through the years, management would inflict their plans on us, they were Q-tips, MOA, SPC, etc.. They spent thousands of dollars on these programs, maybe millions. It was all a waste of time and money, but you couldn't tell him that. When the newsletters first came out, workers would hand them out in the aisle ways, laughing and telling people how good they were. We all had a lot of fun with it and it relieved our stress. Coworkers would spend time drawing out cartoons of their supervisors in a funny way, knowing it would come out in a week or two in the newsletter. The company put a small edition on the plant and got a 12 year tax abatement worth millions from the county. They only added about 10 jobs. And after that 12 years was over they closed the plant, they made the announcement six months after I retired. We had stopped the newsletters 12 years before the plant closed.

I had a couple funny experiences with engineers in the past. One was we were working on this machine trying to get the machine to run and couldn't do it. So the head engineer came out to look at it and couldn't get it running. So I decided to indicate the spindle and found it was not in tolerance so I started to pull it and he came over and said no don't put a new one on there. So I put blueing all over the spindle and closed up of machine. The next day I came in, turned off the machine, opened the machine up and they're was a new spindle, it had been changed. It was running, but that's the way the engineers were they wanted to take credit for everything and they needed it. One time we got new inspection equipment in and nobody had been trained on it so I was over looking at it trying to figure out how to run it, hit the wrong button and out comes a linear graft 3 ½ feet long so I know what button not to push. So one day in comes the head engineer sits down at the machine and acts like he knows what he is doing. Then, as luck would have it. He hit the wrong button and outcomes the 3 ½ foot linear graft. What was funny was the printer started to run. He started to hit other buttons trying to stop it. He must have hit 10 other buttons, punching it as his face grew redder and redder. Finally, when the printer had printed 2 ½ feet. He sat there with his arms crossed, acting like he was waiting for it to end. But I could see he was very uncomfortable as I looked over and smiled not saying a word or course, when the printer stopped. He ripped it off and left immediately, it was amusing.

I learned later that a woman was cheating on the union elections, and cheating me out of serving on the bargaining committee. I guess I made her mad. One day, when the union wanted to have a picnic, which I called a beer party picnic, but they didn't want to do the job on the shop floor to help the workers. So I opposed it, and got the membership to vote against contributing any money to the picnic, and she went off on me, just a part of my job to listen to it, then I walked away. I later learned she cheated on a ratification vote also. We had voted the contract down twice and the third time she cheated and it passed. Now you might ask how I know this. I knew her husband. He was a good man. I'd worked with him for years, when he finally divorced her and it came out later. Of course, nobody wanted to testify to it, so I couldn't do anything about it, but it was a five-year felony for cheating on elections and ratification votes. But I didn't need the union authority to help me to intervene for my co-workers.

Through the years I would take up collections for retirees that had passed away or people that were seriously sick. And what I noticed was an awful lot of people would get cancer. So as time went on we would have discussions around the plant on what we could do about it. One woman said we should have a cancer study, and she knew of someone at the University that did that type of cancer studies. I don't know how we did it, but we got the union to authorize and pay for it. So we all couldn't wait for the results, because we knew that 75 or 80% of the people that retired would come down with some sort of cancer. So as you can probably figure out, time went by and we waited. And we waited, and we knew the cancer study had been completed, but the president of the union refused to release it. Why? So I called the cancer study group and told them I was a Union officer, and I'd like a copy of the cancer study. They said okay, I'll look it up in the files. He came back to the phone and said there's a note on it that only the union president could access copies. He asked me if I was the president. And of course I could have said yes, but I said no. And I didn't get copies. No one ever did. There's more to the story than that. The company went around to everybody that was approaching retirement, and when asked them if they are going to retire this year or next year? They said it was for the actuaries, but I always wondered.

I came into the QA office one day and a coworker was talking about his daughter was missing. And he explained that her ex husband had called and told him that his daughter drove her car over to his house, with the two kids and told him to take care of the kids and he could have the car. So she gave him the keys and drove off with another man. So my coworker was planning a trip to that state to collect her things out of the apartment. He had already called the police and notify them and they've been to the apartment and said it looked like she had run off. So I offered to take up a collection or at least have coworkers pledge

They can take those labels and put them . . . . I feel we should be good Samaritans and help your fellow coworkers when they are in need. As I would want help when I'm in need. I'd like to thank Trafford publishing, and my wife for encouraging me to write this book. It's finally out of my system, and I'm glad I'm retired. May God bless all of you.

money for a reward. He said he would have his wife do the same thing in her workplace. And we can see how much we could come up with. Together, we came up with $5,000 reward. So he notified the police of the reward money and they put out notification of the reward out around the county. After a year, someone came forward, a person that was a friend of someone she knew had done something bad to my coworkers daughter. They hooked her up, and she was to go in and have the people start talking about it. They found out when she drove over there that day, the woman that was living with her ex-husband put the kids in the back bedroom and beat her to death with a hammer. They dragged her body over to a woodpile and burned the body completely up. They did some time in prison, convicted of manslaughter. It was a bad result but at least it brought closure to my coworker, and we were happy to be a part of it.

When the coal miners were on strike in Virginia and West Virginia, we took up a can food drive, and people wanted to give money also. So after we collected over a month or so, the international or at least our region and did the same thing. So we loaded the car up and packed our camping gear and went to Virginia to the coal miners camp and gave them all the supplies and money and set up camp and stayed with them for a few days. They had a large layout of food for breakfast, lunch and dinner. We took tours of the coal mines sights, and met a lot of friends. We went to a Sunday rally of all the coal miners, and it was like a Festival. There must have been 20 or 25,000 people there. It was great. I have been called a communist, a socialist, a revolutionary, a radical, a Democrat, a Republican and other names I can't repeat here but I tell my wife don't call me late to dinner! I never cared about labels.

operator and an inspector most of the time. Now I have six grandchildren that are as cute as can be. I am a life member of the NRA and support gun rights and CCW's. I am a life member of the North American hunting club. I use to hunt, golf and garden, but I can't anymore because of health reasons. I'm a patent holder. And finally, I wrote this book. It was my dream. I love retirement, thank you and may God bless!

About the author:

I've worked every job since I was 10 years old that I could get. I started scab—caddying, raking leaves, cutting grass, shoveling snow, painting, delivering papers. At 14 I got a work permit and started working at a printing shop in town and started working as a caddie at a posh country club on the weekends. At 16 I had enough money for a car. The insurance ,the licenses and I started working at a grocery store, bagging groceries, cashiering and stocking shelves. I graduated from high school and had a graduating class of over 1100. We lived in a big 10 college town with about 200,000 people. I went to college for 2 ½ years at a community college. And I worked full time, all the while, I drove a cab and was a security guard and a desk sergeant. I was against the war in Vietnam and got a 4-F medical deferment. I was a meditator, the Maharishi,TM, God bless him. I met my wife of 40 years. She was a coal miner's daughter. We had four children, and we lived by the lake, while we raised the kids. We enjoyed boating, swimming and fishing and campfires. I got a job that had insurance and benefits at the bearing factory. I served as a union steward for years and was on the bargaining committee. In the plant I worked as a janitor, operator, set up, furnace